# Quantum Healing
# SECRETS

## For More Energy, Vitality and Momentum Every Day of Your Life

D1134048

## Julie Renee

# ALSO BY JULiE RENEE

## Books

Your Divine Human Blueprint
- 100% You Formula
- Quantum Healing Secrets
- Awakening the Healthy Human
- Balance Your Life Now
- Breaking Through
- Illumination

## Programs

- More than 150 trainings on all areas of full self-expression and the use of quantum activations
- Julie Renee's Year of Miracles
- Diamond Ambassador Certification & Training
- Quantum Activation Apprentice Certification & Training Meditations

• 187 meditations on all topics for full self-expression health regeneration love and wealth building

## Music

• Gratitude: India classical influence harp and vocals
• Pleasures: Celtic harp and vocals
• The Message: Rumi Love Poetry
• Illumination: Harp

## App

• Q5 Quantum Meditations in 5 minutes!

All are available online, you may order by visiting
http://julierenee.com/programs/

# TABLE OF CONTENTS

## Module Two: Three Secrets of Miraculous Healing and Building New Cells

## Module Three: DNA and Stem Cell Regeneration

## Module Four: Restore Balance and Joy to Your Life

## Module Five: vision

# YOUR iNTRODUCTiON TO QUANTUM HEALiNG SECRETS

The Quantum healing shifts you are moving towards are not about luck: it's really about Science. Sure, everyone is different but the same laws of success always apply. You reap what you sow; you can't get out of life what you are not willing to put into it. If you want more love, give more love. If you want greater success, help others achieve more. And when you study and master the science of achievement, you will find the success you desire.

The Content provided in this book supports your mastering the mindset necessary for Improving, maintaining, and sustaining health over a lifetime. You'll find the full home study course Quantum Healing Success on my website JulieRenee.com. The chapters in this book will support your journey back to good health and enduring vitality. What I hope you receive is a reset to build a mindset for unlimited possibility.

Understand that your decisions shape your destiny. The future is what you make of it. Every day of your life little decisions will either take you to the life you desire or to disaster by default. In fact, it is the littlest decisions that shape your life.

## What to Expect in the Pages of This Book

I have included stories and step-by-step guides in nine specific areas: Brain, Rejuvenation, DNA, Hormones, Vision, Dynamic Energy, Pain, Love Regeneration and Rejuvenation. Some people experience a shift instantly just by reading and enjoying the content while others grow gradually into the upgrades over time using the home study and one to one VIP experience. This is meant to be an overview and really to support your mindset for optimal shifts.

When thinking about using Quantum Healing Secrets to effect change, a good rule of thumb is to know that if you came to read the book or participate in the home study program with many health, love and or work issues—this may not be enough to get you to where you want to be. The more challenges you had coming in, the more shifts and changes need to ground for your full restoration.

There are 3 types of people who look to this kind of a program to experience rejuvenation

1. Already well, perhaps in a healing profession—wanting more out of life and looking to get the slight edge over themselves —being able to out perform their status quo and reach for the stars.

2. Doing fine but noticing physical and emotional challenges as well as cognitive decline—in other words, your body and brain are no longer giving you what you needed and wanted.

3. The third type of individual comes in with a wealth of issues, many of them related to health and a real desire to make rapid improvements. These people have already tried many healing modalities with little luck and have ended up here looking to change their health status now by participating in this quantum home study program as a last and best hope. If you are in this position understand that your journey back

is different than a healthy person. Years have gone by with issues that have made life difficult, and you will have a gradual journey back. The trick here is to first restore hope. This is not a 'get rich healthy quick scheme.' But rather a scientifically proven method for restoring health by literally regenerating the cellular body a step at a time.

Your biggest job going through the program is to affirm that you can indeed get the concepts and ideas taught and that you are indeed capable of healing and getting better. Stay in gratitude and appreciation for what is working in your life and your body every minute of every day. If you are telling yourself every minute how awful everything is, it will be difficult to experience any shifts—ever. That doesn't mean they aren't happening, as a matter of fact, they are. However, you may, with your mindset, enforce an inability to use more than a very diminished percentage in spite of the high capacity. Remember the old adage, what the mind can believe and conceive it will achieve. It works both ways; what the mind focuses on good or bad is where you will go.

Follow all the suggested guidelines below as if your life depended on it, and please find ways to celebrate life and have fun every day!

Meditation is an important part of every training I provide, so I am including a meditation success guide here at the beginning of the book. Even if you are new to meditation, this guide will give you what you need to be successful from the start.

# PEMER: THE HUMAN BLUEPRiNT

## Perception

To start living your powerful, enduring, wealthy, happy and in-love-with-your-life "life," you'll need to clean house in your perception. This includes your mindset, emotions, influential group mind and thought forms. You need to open to your biggest, best self to allow the vision of the Quantum Mind to permeate all parts of you.

Here's why it's so important: Once you've achieved a level of clarity, focus and momentum, you'll want to support that process with a healthy lifestyle. If you've been living with a perception that is not entirely yours, it means that you are living an inauthentic life. It weakens your voice in the world. It weakens your power and your impact with others. Imagine setting yourself into that special category of people who are living life, not only full on, but who are totally in charge of all aspects of life. In essence, you become the director of your own journey.

Everything is possible. There are no limitations just endless possibilities.

## Essence

The second part of your Divine Human Blueprint for restoring your unstoppable Quantum Mind and life is your Essence. Take a moment and feel into your spirit. Spirit is you—your essence— that which comes with you, whether you are in or out of the body.

You don't have to be religious to understand the workings of your spirit. If you are religious or spiritual, what I am going to tell you next may surprise you. Your Human Essence is comprised of three important elements: Human Spirit, Soul and Life force.

1. **Human Spirit** needing care and repair from time to time. Essence is, as described earlier, that which is with you whether you are in or out of your body. It is your light, your information, your presence.

2. **Human Soul.** We have in our culture mistakenly used the word, "soul," to describe spirit. Your soul is different than spirit. Your soul is the protective chalice of spirit. It is like a thick skin surrounding and protecting your light. It wanes or reduces in strength and size when you are unwell or under attack.

3. **Life force.** Though you might have imagined life force as part of your energy body, it does indeed belong in Human Essence. When your life force is low, you will feel weak. Simply by pumping your life force up using a quantum energy technique, your strength, vitality and energy can come right back. Literally, this reversal can happen in a matter of minutes.

## Matter

Matter is the human body, cells, glands, and organs, and the fluid, bones, and ligaments that form the body you live in. Let me say clearly: It doesn't matter what shape you are in, physically or otherwise. There are a set of principles, keys and practices that surround living in a human body. You were created with an accessible design and were meant to be able to "self-diagnose and self-restore."

YOU HAVE TO OWN YOUR BRAIN AND BODY COM-PLETELY. You have to then own and live in your body—cells, glands, and organs—100%. And finally, to really get to the place where you can be fully in charge and powerful, you have to be the Quantum Mindset that supports your healthy body. This includes your brain, nervous system, and all other systems, glands, organs, and every part of you that forms what we call, "matter." This is your ticket to freedom and a life fully empowered.

Using the Divine Human Blueprint, your brain and body will be a primary source of joy and empowerment for you. You'll have the opportunity to up-level your health to the highest human potential. Feeling great all the time, and being able to access the Divine Human Blueprint when something seems to be off, will give you an unstoppable and unending advantage in work, home, family, and love. Most importantly, your quantum mindset and healthy body will be the access point for going deeper into the fulfillment of your dreams. Wealth, fame, contribution, finding your soulmate, investing, running a marathon, becoming a marketing master or a bestselling author—whatever your big dreams are—they can only happen when your Quantum mindset and 100% healthy body can support your future vision.

When you are in charge of and 'own,' your matter (matter comprises all parts of your physical body), if you are an entrepreneur or business person (or want to be), you have something very powerful to bring to the table. You can actually offer your gifts in tangible and manifested ways, because you are physically and fully present; you are really there.

Don't let impatience or a "hurry up" mentality get the better of you. This can take you out of the game so fast. There is enough time, energy, and love to get you back to you. By pacing yourself, you are telling yourself there is no emergency, that you are not on high alert, and that you will not be moving onto the next new thing if this doesn't work. Instead, you are living naturally with the knowledge that you are changing, your mind is working better and you are growing healthier and younger with each passing day. You trust in the Universe. You trust in your body to restore itself.

Once you have established great health, quantum mindset, and increased your energy, you will naturally go deeper into the fulfillment of your life's purpose and mission in the most meaningful and creative ways. You will be operating from a vantage point of being fully funded, and your own energetic field will support you like never before.

## Energy

Once you have the right mindset and emotions in place, your perception has shifted, you've gathered a possibly fragmented Spirit, Soul and reduced Life Force and brought it back up to 100% and you've accessed the Divine Human Blueprint formula to restore all aspects of the physical body (matter) to its very, very best self, what's the next step?

The final step is all about getting your energy up to your peak performance. You need energy. You always need to have energy fueling your body. And it's easy when you know the simple steps to make it happen.

Our spirit informs our DNA, even as we are cells dividing in our mother's womb, as to how to set up the game of life. Our life force activates as we separate from our mother's life force at the time of our birth. Once perception and essence are made right, matter—the human body in all its complexity—must be addressed. Finally, our energy body, and the fuel we need to keep our physical body alive, is addressed. Energy is originally designed by spirit programming, sent into the DNA and grown after the body emerges from the passage of birth. The energy body develops largely in the first seven years of life. Energy Includes: chakras, aura, golden rings, meridians, nadies and human spirit access portal.

Now we get to realms and bring the work out of theory into reality.

## Realms

The fifth aspect of the 100% Healthy Divine Human Blueprint is divided into four unique areas, each related to the other. You will see why we have them lumped together as I explain more to you.

The Realms affecting humanity are unseen and powerfully influential.

The four Realms are:

1. Genesis is where we came from and starts from the beginning of humanity. This realm dates back to original perception even before human spirit. This realm encompasses both historical and pure truth. It cannot be altered, as it just plainly "is." It is our guidepost and a true Omega. It is our record, our history of fulfillment.

2. Amplification is, in effect, like ripples emanating from a pebble thrown into a pond, yet far more powerful. In this expanding realm, not unlike our expanding universe, more is possible. This realm is related also to Genesis. It is spontaneous. It is a realm that is ultimately the precursor to energy.

3. Quantum is the realm of no time, no space, connection, and oneness. Human mastery provides a powerful quantum field surrounding the master—altering, bending, shifting, eliminating, and moving through time, space, health, wealth, love and all things we can imagine. It includes all things beyond imagination.

4. Embodiment is what allows us as human spirit to take form in a human body. The normal way to experience the realm of embodiment is to be born as an infant to parents. Some

yogis are able to move in and out of the realm of embodiment, taking their corporeal bodies with them into different fields of existence, and return, appearing the same as when they left us.

Truthfully, you don't really need to know much about the realms, very little in fact, to activate the Divine Human Blueprint and get yourself going in the direction of your "100% healthy, happy, wealthy, and in-love-with-your-life" life. The realms support the Blueprint as you may have already noticed. Most importantly, to understand the realms, notice in the area of perception, if there is anything that is getting in the way of you having a full, rich relationship with each of them. In other words, are you limited in being supported by one, or all of them, based on programs in perception or elsewhere in the Divine Human Blueprint? If so, these are areas you will correct.

To me, the combined information of the realms is really the magic chalice that supports your healthy body and life.

**Note:** the more you activate the Blueprint, in other words, focus your intentions on the full experience of the 100% Healthy formula, the more rapidly things in your life will improve. Talk about walking around and sparkling… you will become a bright beacon of light, guiding all your dreams to you effortlessly.

The Divine Human Blueprint will literally kick start your vitality, your career, and your love life, all at once. It will save you months or even years of struggle, instead of going endlessly from one health practitioner, business coach or therapist until you are overwhelmed with hopelessness and exhaustion. Instead, you will live and breathe in the light of blessedness and grace.

How much is that worth to you?

# SiMPLE STEPS TO MEDiTATiON  SUCCESS

Tried to meditate with no luck? You may be missing a few key details that will take you from failure to success. World renowned meditation expert and miraculous healer Julie Renee shares her secrets on making your meditation   unstoppable.

## About Meditation

The style of meditation I teach to my students begins with grounding and clearing tools. Then, we progress through steps to bring ease, focus, and vibrant health to the practitioner. Meditation is a lifetime practice.

I have provided numerous guided meditation programs on all topics for regeneration healing, stress, love and wealth. Even reversing aging is possible in the Beauty program for women as well as stem cell regeneration and DNA removal! You'll find these by going to Julie Renee.com/meditation

## How to Be Unstoppable in Your Meditation Practice: Letting Go of Failed Behaviors

Avoid the hurried and scattered "grab a few minutes here or there" approach. When beginning a practice that will benefit you for a lifetime you need to make a commitment.

Find a regular time each day you can devote to your spiritual growth, regardless of other demands or priorities. This may mean you wake up earlier every day to meditate for twenty minutes before the kids are stirring or routine responsibilities are calling (or prior to bed or during lunch time)? Consider what is best for you and commit to it for 90 days—adjust if necessary, but honor your promise to yourself. Give yourself a high level of permission to enjoy and experience your personal and spiritual growth!

Here are some things to avoid, and best practices:

1. Avoid: Meditating in an ungrounded or active space. Best: You want to find a spot (in your home or garden preferably) where you will meditate every day. The energy of this space is dedicated to your spiritual pursuits and self-calming. You can still fulfill your daily practice when travelling. Carry a meditation cushion or a 12"X 18" piece of white wool which will become infused with your energy, and remember to ground and own the room for yourself.

2. Avoid: Eating a big meal just prior to meditation. Oops! Food in the tummy is a big distraction. Best: A common practice if you feel you need nourishment is to have a cup of Chai or a small amount of fresh fruit so you remain in the bliss zone. Heavy meals will draw the blood and prana (life force energy) out of your head and into your lower chakras; meditation is about lifting up into the upper chakras and enjoying the seven chakras above your head. This is so much fun when all the energies are in sync!

3. Avoid: Sitting in an uncomfortable position or feeling chilled or too warm. Best: Intentionally create a beautiful, simple space. Experienced yogis and yoginis enjoy   a

meditation shawl and cushion, but it is just as appropriate to sit upright in a chair with a cozy afghan wrap. Remember, these are dedicated moments of special connection with your sacred self. Give yourself permission to be completely comfortable and supported. When dealing with chronic pain, and in this case only, lying meditation is a good choice. I don't recommend this posture for others because lying down is the position for sleep so it then becomes sleep, not meditation... of course sleep is wonderful and necessary but that is not the goal of meditation. Those who choose the lying down form must be extra diligent to stay present and alert!

4. Avoid: Self-criticism and perfect pictures. Ouch! These are the pictures of having to "be perfect," getting it right, or expecting to be an expert immediately or during every meditation session. If you tell yourself you can't meditate, then you will fulfill that command, but let me reassure you that everyone can meditate.

Best: It's like exercising a muscle—the more often you work out, the stronger your muscles get. Likewise the more you practice meditation—the key word here being "practice" (not "perfect")—the stronger and easier your practice will become. Remind yourself you are in the learning/adapting phase and that you love the sacred time spent in meditation.

I provide you with beautiful guidance on the meditation tapes. Within a few days or weeks you will remember all the steps and we can enhance your personalized meditation program.

Relax, enjoy, and have fun. This is not serious stuff. It is the fuel for bliss, happiness and deep connection with yourself, the god of your heart and all others! How wonderful for you to have come to a place in your journey where you can receive this gift of self-love, care and awareness!

# MEDiTATiON: i AM SAFE iN PRESENT TiME

Take a deep breath in and relax. Begin to feel your body surrender to the softness of meditation. If you can, allow your eyes to slowly drift shut and relax. Send a grounding cord down from the base of your spine to the center of the earth; make it nice and wide and release all the stress and tension from the day week, month and year. You are safe. Release your male or female body, grounding and clearing as we go.

See your adrenal glands in your mind's eye. They are acorn shaped glands about two inches off the spine and an inch or so up from the waist. Ground each of your adrenals with a line of energy as wide as your wrist hollow in the center down to the base of the spine (first chakra) and then down to the center of the earth. Set the adrenals on release and begin to release all the stress/fight or flight energy from the adrenals. Let go of tension and totally relax.

Draw a line between the sciatic nerve to the adrenal grounding and imagine grounding and releasing your entire nervous system through the adrenals. Release the congestion, gunky goopy build-up of tar-like energy (if you have it) from your nervous system. Continue to relax and let go.

Ground a line of energy from the center of your head (close to your brain stem) and first brain (the reptilian brain). Press an imaginary release button at the bottom of the brain stem. Release the congested, reactive, darting energy of the first brain down through the first chakra. Send the pent up energy down to the center of the earth.

Invite your emotional brain, (the second brain that wraps around the first brain) to release through the same grounding cord. Let go of emotional tensions and thoughts of stress or impending doom.

Allow the stored memories that have negatively affected your feelings of safety a place to surface as black dots in the brain. Using a golden vacuum cleaner, vacuum up the black dots. Bring a golden sun to the top of your head and fill in all the newly cleared places in the body with Gold. Affirm that you are safe, secure and all is now well in your wonderful world.

Open your feet chakras to earth energy running energy up through your feet, ankles, shins, calves, knees, and thighs out the hips and down the grounding chord. Bring in universal energy through the back of your head, down your neck and shoulders, out the arms and finger tips as well as down through your back channels, looping back up through the pelvic cradle, up the belly through the chest, neck and head, fountaining out the top of the head, cleansing your aura.

Pull your aura into your body about 36 inches from your skin. Make sure the aura has a sharp, defined edge to it. Place your protection rose at the front edge of your aura and ground it to the center of the earth.

Bring a golden sun to the top of your head; see yourself as a spirit sitting peacefully, ready to come fully back into your body.

Give yourself the validation you richly deserve; you are safe lovable and loving, you are strong, healthy, vibrant, beautiful, wise and strong.

Bring yourself as a spirit back into your body along with this golden sun, filled with validation. Breathe in and out several times deeply feeling energized and renewed ready to face your life with a restored sense of safety. May it be with the blessings of the supreme being that this healing meditation is complete!

Welcome back!

Personal meditations and healings in a one to one setting during session time also address our family patterns, through DNA clearings, our present life, timelines as well as clearing stored emotions in other parts of the physical body, and past life influences.

The benefit to this meditation is that it allows you to experience present time, joys and happiness without the weight of fears and worries to overshadow your present moment's issues.

Joy and happiness, peace and love, that's my theme; the more, the better!

# MODULE ONE:
## BRAIN

# BRAiN REGENERATiON FROM STEM CELLS

As the number one brain rejuvenation expert, I'm very excited to see the transformations we are getting with improved brain function in both capacity and use for clients and students. The unique process of brain regeneration is done through a technique that I developed over the last seven years working with the individual own stem cells and the quantum field.

## The Brain

The brain is an organ that serves as the center of the nervous system enclosed in the cranium serving to control and coordinate the mental and physical actions of the human body.

Brain regeneration involves a six-step process. The results are consistent though we see a variance in how much the individual is able to incorporate. When an individual is very ill there is a longer projection for addressing related issues and system wide challenges. Each illness or malady with its own unique causes may be resolved by following the procedures laid out in the protocols found in Your Divine Human Blueprint.

Brain regeneration does not change your personality and in itself does not make you smarter. What it does do is raise the set point of surviving, learning, emotional ease, creativity, understanding logic and problem solving and access to your own genius to 100%. What that means is with brain regeneration you can learn and grow without the limits you were born with.

> ...Improving your brain capacity includes the removal of programs that first caused the brain to malfunction.
> —Julie Renee

First we remove soul contracts, demonic curses, group mind, (memes) group mind virus, (miasma) black magic, curses, traumatic episodes from past lives, emotional programs and finally DNA. With the exception of DNA you might think of these programs as powerful thought forms negatively influencing our being. Once these programs are completely cleared out, the individual is ready for regeneration.

**Step 1** involves clearing the large group of thought forms along with step two DNA obliteration—the removal of harmful or negative DNA programs must be completed prior to regeneration for it to hold. For example if you had a program for dementia in your DNA and left it there—it would still lay in wait to spring up at some future date.

**Step 2** is brain regeneration. **Step 3** is the removal of all dark energies and spiritual parasites. Spiritual parasites are the topic of an entire book, so suffice it to say—just like the unseen dust mites that live in your eyelashes—there are entities and the like that inhabit body and brain. We clear these out using the quantum field. The experience is usually very pleasant.

**Step 4** is cell regeneration. The proper name for this step is Cellular Neo Genesis, which is a process that requires working with the master cell—one brain at a time.

Starting with brain on the survival brain (also referred to as the reptilian brain) using the quantum field we bring the master cell to 100% God state.

The process might be understood better by thinking of an image of a torn leaf. Using Kirlian photography you will also see the image of the torn away part of the leaf. It still exists. You've likely also heard of amputees having phantom limb pain. It's because the limb and the emotional trauma related to the limb have continued to exist. The human blueprint in its perfected state exists as an accessible template from which regeneration is possible.

**Step 5** involves mirroring the healthy master stem cells to all surrounding cells. Amplified with gold energy this helps the fatigued and low functioning cells take a big step up and function at a much higher level.

**Step 6** is where the magic and transformation is amplified. Up till now we have used the quantum field to clear and restore we use the field of genesis in the restoration of cells and finally in step six we use the field of amplification to promote the cascade of new cell growth. This process is stimulated by activating a program for regeneration of cells in the mitochondria.

Part of this process is to mirror the healthy 100% restored stem cells to the surrounding cells. This mirroring delivers a big boost to all the surrounding cells. The mitochondria are the fuel generator of the cell and it is in this part of the cell where the program for regeneration is contained. This mechanism supports us to begin a cascade of cell growth. From brain regenerations inception we were originally getting 70 to 90 days of cell growth and years latter we are witnessing cell growth up to 150 days. This is an extraordinary breakthrough from which the client, whether healthy and alert to begin with or a traumatic brain injury survivor experiences profound and very deep shifts and changes. We have created a foundation for incredible renewal and revitalization!

Steps 4, 5 and 6 are repeated in each brain.

Survival Reptilian

Emotional

Creative

Logical and

Genius

One of the most popular results of this generation is the quiet mind balancing; Participants experience a deep peace and a new 'emotional generosity.' Life continues to happen with it's ups and downs yet people who have gone through the brain rejuvenation process experience an incredible sense of well-being regardless of their circumstances. Most folks are 100 times more able and ready to cope with the challenges that arise with a sense of ease.

Additional benefits include more brainpower to solve problems and expanded sense of creativity and divine connection, clarity and sharper focus, as everything in life seems to works better. The freshly (grown) brain finds excitement in learning—it's easier to grasp new concepts and ideas. Life becomes more enjoyable as the 100% brain capacity returns the individual to their natural divine intelligence.

Brain regeneration is truly the wave of the future and is for everyone. If you think about being a child—your brain is constantly growing and making brain leaps—why would we want this to end in our 20s and live with a brain that no longer gets stronger and smarter? This technique allows you to regenerate and if properly nurtured will continue to improve for up to 20 years! Imagine your bright future. We are using both cellular neo genesis and DNA obliteration to successfully grow 'new brains' for every participant with 100% capacity as the final result for each and every participant.

Now that you can picture the stem cell existing in your own blueprint envision the quantum field applied to the cell, we see amazing results with this simple and very effective technique. Because the blueprint exists regardless of outer appearances in what we call matter (all the physical components of the human design), we are able to use a unique process called Cellular Neo Genesis to bring the damaged or missing master stem cells back to it's 100% "God" state.

A great example of cellular neo genesis is Holly who had a PET scan during cancer treatments that showed she had a failed adrenal the size of a raisin no longer functioning and according to medical science, failed forever with no hope of growing back. Upon applying quantum field energy to the master cells of her failed adrenal, we were able to produce a cascade of new cell growth and ultimately grow to full size and function her failed adrenal. Her radiologist medically documented this four months after the first certification of the failed adrenal.

Once the regeneration of the individual master cell is successfully completed we use a program in the mitochondria to begin the cascade of new cell growth. For every gland organ or system there are numbers unique to each of days of regeneration. The average days for growing an adrenal back are about 42. In contrast the brain 135 days and the thyroid 72 days of new cell growth.

This last example Cellular Neo Genesis was with an existing gland. In this case we found stem cells at extreme low function. The other versions of cellular neo genesis are of an entirely missing gland or organ. We see this when a surgical procedure removes entirely the gland or organ. Although we have not yet gotten consistent results from this procedure everyone who has gone through the process has experienced improvements. We use the identical technique to the one we use when a body part is damaged or extremely low in function.

I think of my own tonsils and which were surgically removed at age 3 and grown back 43 years later to full adult size—in a short amount of time. A more impressive example is our dear Carolyn who had her colon removed and was dying from seven infections in the abdominal area. Her procedure began with  removing a. death energy, b. 7 infections and c. repairing the leaky gut by building cells in the large and small intestines. Caroline's health dramatically improved and her desire was to have the colostomy bag removed so she might return to a normal relationship with her husband and a happy family life experience. With focused attention to her colon in the divine blueprint we were able to begin the process of cellular neo genesis and successfully grow back her colon over a period of time. Her personal goal of having the colostomy bag removed was realized and she is living a comfortable, happy, healthy life in wine country. Her doctors warned if they removed the bag she would suffer constantly from explosive uncontrollable diarrhea. Carolyn has never experienced a moment of discomfort and experiences a normal digestive process.

Working with stem cells is an exciting experience whether you are using a potent product like Swisscell (which is an oral stem cell supplement) improving vitality and longevity—made by my dear friend Burton Goldberg or you are in the leading edge of scientific research like Professor Jerry Crabtree my dear friend at Stanford. And one of our Quantum Healing students Bill Obrien who is bringing stem cell technology to burn victims all over the planet with his incredible serums—what we all are excited about is both potential and results! Everyone working with stem cells knows the untapped and incredible regenerative power to be experienced with proper activation of stem cells to the body.

SIMPLE AND EASY: Using the quantum field to restore stem cells is the effective way to regenerate the body, skin, glands and organs. Humanity is ready to experience health, vibrancy and full energy with a bright and exciting future in store for everyone. Stem cell research is truly the wave of the future and we are so delighted to be presenting the easier, faster, more direct way to activate your stem cells. What's so extraordinary about these breakthroughs are that they are already part of your original design and it is what you were gifted so you could naturally stay young and healthy for many years to come.

# GET RiD OF "FUZZY BRAiN"
# WiTH THE 'SiP SiXTEEN' SYSTEM

## Your Brain Can't Store Water.
## What Does Dehydration Cost Your Body and Business?

The cause of fuzzy brain—the inability to remember names, important details, calculate, and even produce symptoms of ADD in healthy adults—could be just as simple as not drinking water at the proper intervals during the day.

You are losing about 80 ounces of water daily through breathing, sweating and peeing. If you are in the norm, you are drinking 32 ounces of water daily. The cost of dehydration could be the difference between success and failure!

When I say "fuzzy brain," what comes to mind? Lost momentum, unclear thinking, or the inability to follow through on a plan of action? Does it signal a sense of hopelessness in you that you will never accomplish your mission in the world? Does it stimulate depression or anxiety? Perhaps you know your brain could be different, but your outer evidence does not seem to be lining you up for a powerful win.

Fuzzy brain is not your fault, but the cure may be so much easier then you realize.

In my research I have discovered millions of Americans are experiencing cognitive decline—in other words, their brains are increasingly not performing their tasks well.

I became interested in the brain because I've had the worst brain problems that you can imagine. I've had two traumatic brain injuries and, to add insult to injury, as a child I survived atomic bomb exposure. As a result, I ended up with multiple cancers, 17 surgeries, and death itself. Being profoundly ill, taking prescribed medications and radiation poisoning are not good for the brain. I'm here to tell you, even if you've been to hell and back, your brain can give you 100% function all day long!

I've had brain function as bad as it gets and it's the reason why I developed a process to remedy fuzzy brain. What I discovered in my research is that once the brain is up to 100% function, all areas of health and life can rise to 100% and hold there. In this article, I won't be able to give you the full 500-page dissertation I wrote on how applying quantum energy can upgrade your brain function to 100%, but I will give you the most important and simplest step you can implement today to get your brain working so much better.

## Let's Talk About Proper Hydration

Are you a guzzler (meaning you guzzle 8–16 ounces of water after not drinking anything for 4 or 5 hours)? Or are you a sipper? If you're a sipper you drink 4 ounces every 30 minutes all day long. By the way, hydration is water intake, not coffee or green tea, which serves to dehydrate you.

If you are only 1 percent dehydrated, you will likely have a 5 percent decrease in cognitive function. If your brain drops 2 percent in body water, you may suffer from fuzzy short-term memory, inability to focus and have trouble calculating. Know that dehydration is linked to attention deficit in healthy people.

Imagine the long-term toll on your brain if you starve yourself of proper hydration for years. Could this be a factor in the rising numbers of people who are being affected by Dementia and Alzheimer's?

Are you now convinced that you need to change your drinking habits? Do you want to know the best way to do so?

## The Sip Sixteen System

Water must be taken into your body in its pure, natural state. Optimally, you will drink half your body weight in ounces daily. For example, if you are 130 pounds, drink 65 ounce of water. If you were drinking this in 4-ounce increments, you would take sixteen 4-ounce water enhancements daily. I call this the 'sip sixteen system'.

## The Miracle of Water in the Body and Brain

Water gives the brain the electrical energy for all brain functions, including thought and memory processes. If you experience memory lapses, drink more water. Water is vital to energy production in your cells and in your overall metabolism, production of hormones, nerve function and neurotransmission.

When your brain is functioning on a full reserve of water, and you've taken in sixteen 4-ounce water enhancements with the 'sip sixteen' system, you will be able to think faster, be more focused, and experience greater clarity and creativity all day long.

If you suffer from fuzzy brain, you've lost hundreds of hours of productive, clear focused work time. I challenge you to follow the simple 'sip sixteen' system for the next 21 days and watch your fuzzy brain disappear. Good health and better brain function are already within you. The choice is yours: how good do you want to feel?

# iMPLEMENTiNG THE "SiP SiXTEEN METHOD" FOR PROPER HYDRATiON

## Getting the Horse to Drink

You can lead a horse to water… now what's the trick to getting him to drink properly? When faced with the daunting task of drinking 65 to 90 ounces of water daily, most folks go into overwhelm and become hopeless in action.

They revert quickly to their old dehydration habits and return to fuzzy brain headaches and fatigue, despite their awareness that the simple act of drinking 4 ounces of water every half hour would produce immeasurable positive results.

## Getting the Horse to Water

Educating and getting the horse fired up and motivated is the first task in the transformation to better focus, clarity and function for your healthy, happy brain.

Have you ever really thought about what it's costing you to not stay hydrated? Are you losing work time? Struggling with a dark, fuzzy or achy brain? Do you routinely battle fatigue, poor hormone and brain chemistry, or nervous issues? Is your metabolism in the dumper? All of these issues are dramatically improved through proper hydration.

Want to make this a permanent change? I have found that by looking at it more closely—not just thinking about it, but by writing about it—you can help make the change stick. Take out a pen and paper and write down what it's costing you to not stay hydrated all day long.

Are you missing the mark with financial goals? Not bringing your best self to relationships? Where are you out of focus and failing?

Awareness – having clarity about what it's costing you is the first step. Change can only happen when you are awake to the real cost of any issue.

Now imagine being fully energized, focused and clear. What could you produce? How would your relationships be different? How would your life change?

Great! Now you've got the possibilities flowing. Are you at the water trough? LOL!

## Okay, Now That You Are Motivated, What's Next?

I have found that when you look at 80 ounces of water, related to the 5 bottles you need to polish off during the course of a day, most people go into a freak out mode. "I can't possibly drink that much. I'll be running to the bathroom all day."

Let's address that.

If you are a guzzler—meaning you wait 3 or 4 hours, then guzzle down 16 ounces, yes, you will pee out a lot of that water. That's because you have flooded your system; you've absorbed between 4-8 ounces and the rest gets flushed.

If, however, you follow the "Sip Sixteen Method," you are now drinking 4 ounces every 30–45 minutes all day long. This method allows you to replace the water you are losing at the proper pace, so that you will no longer spend all that extra time running to the bathroom.

For my VIP sessions, I provide a craft of water with a small 5-ounce glass for my clients, allowing the drinking process to become simple, easy, and effortless. Clients surprise themselves as they go through carafes without noticing any difficulty.

Drinking this way is psychologically doable and brilliantly rewarding. Try the "Sip Sixteen System" by providing yourself with visual cues that make your ability to stay hydrated truly possible. You will change your hydration habits for the rest of your life.

# BRAiN DRAiN: SiDE EFFECTS OF
# 25 YEARS ON THE WORLD WiDE WEB

Happy twenty-fifth birthday WWW. With more users then ever surfing the net, working long hours online, and spending leisure time 'plugged in' one wonders how many new maladies have arisen from the age of technology?

With large numbers of daily users on for hours at a time, as a 100% brain regeneration expert I see three pitfalls most adults fall into and some simple solutions to cure brain drain and get us back celebrating the birth of the web.

## Three Pitfalls of World Wide Web Brain Drain

Sleep
Sight
Spirit

**Sleep disorders** are rapidly rising to the forefront of source cause for poor productivity and performance in the work place. **Problem:** if you are one of the many evening computer users like my dear friend Barbara, a busy working actress and media trainer, you will lose the healthy function of your pineal gland by staring into a night computer screen during the sunset hours, fooling the body that daylight is continuing and preventing the natural release of the sleep hormone melatonin. Cure: turn off the computer by 7 pm. Instead of doing computer work you can read a book, visit with friends or head off to a bubble bath, get an early sleep or some intimate lovemaking. This is sure to add balance and, over time, get you sleeping naturally once more.

Sight problems are accelerated with long dehydrating hours starring into a computer screen. Problem: As your eyes dehydrate the lens hardens and the vision worsens. Cure: Stay hydrated by drinking four ounces of water every half hour. As you take your water break, stand up move to a window with a pretty view—breathe deeply and dance wildly for 90 seconds.

Drinking pure, clean water gets the brain and eyes hydrated; looking at beauty restores the human spirit to the eyes~ protecting the eyes from damage and the dancing moves you out of trance into self.

Which leads us to our third and final S~ spirit. Problem: Human spirit seems to disappear for the most part from the body as technology uses primarily the reptilian and logical brains to support functions and tasks normal to most computer users. Ever notice how disconnected you feel after a prolonged session on the web? While parts of your brain are engaged you also lose one major brain wave as you trance out. Spending many hours on the computer seems to go hand in hand with relationship skill issues and the interruption of spiritual growth. Cure: Take your regular breaks including water, viewing beauty and 90 seconds of dancing, and add deep breathing into your routine. Close your eyes, breathing in pink and gold light, and breathing out stale stressful energy; repeat ten cycles.

A few final tips to get you right with your technology: Remind yourself you are not a machine, keep life in balance—adding time for friends, fun and time in nature as your way of life. Daily meditation will give the brain and body an internal cleanse from the inside out.

Being your best and getting the best out of the World Wide Web requires thoughtfulness and strategy. But what in life that is worth anything doesn't? Happy surfing, sleeping, and celebrating 25 years of World Wide Web connection!

# SiR ANTHONY HOPKiNS REvEALS BRAiNCHALLENGES

From a learning disability to outrageous success: What I learned from Sir Anthony is common sense and easy to implement. How do you get those dreams off the shelf and put your fabulous life in motion?

I had the extreme pleasure to meet with Sir Anthony Hopkins in LA recently. When I posted the photo of Anthony and me on Facebook, I received oodles of responses from the female community. Turns out Sir Anthony is the object of affection, admiration, and innocent fantasy among my fellow female Facebook devotees.

From my work with children over the years who suffer from autism, depression, ADD and ADHD, Anthony's life story was compelling and had me appreciate him and his perseverance to success all the more

Anthony relayed a story of his young life and the difficulties he experienced in school. He had poor grades, was really tried, and struggled to get through. He was told he would fail in life and never amount to much. Yet, Sir Anthony Hopkins is truly one of the most beloved, talented, and popular male actors of his age group—or for that matter—any age group.

He spoke of his dream to be an actor and how much he wanted it. He disregarded the predictions of a poor to mediocre life and worked very, very hard to accomplish his dream of being a successful actor.

Anthony is a great example of overcoming enormous obstacles and making a wondrous life for himself. Truly, the fulfillment of his goal has literally given great joy and amusement to millions of moviegoers.

Children no longer have to struggle and suffer with learning and brain challenges. The One to One VIP program offers real help, no drugs or behavior modification.

Have you left your big dreams on a shelf?

The trouble today is that people are content to let their dreams rest on the shelf.

Blaming the economy or the lack of skill and time to implement, our society has lost its luster for fulfilling the American dream.

How do you get those dreams off the shelf and put your dream life in motion? What I learned from Sir Anthony is common sense and easy to implement.

You have to see it, feel it down to your bones, taste it, want it, and at all cost, go for it. Overcoming an obstacle means amplifying your talents and putting on the gas!

Take action. Get the training and be seen. Anthony's big break came in his Oscar winning role as Hannibal Lecter in **Silence of the Lambs**. By that time, he had been in action for years fulfilling his life's passion.

# MiCHAEL PHELPS STRUGGLES
# WiTH ADHD AND DEPRESSiON

The most decorated Olympian in US history, competing currently in the 2012 London Olympic games, was locked out of the medals in his first race of these games. Perhaps his bout with depression affected this result. Michael Phelps stated he has used his athletic and swimming vocation to channel the intensity of childhood ADHD. After the last Olympic competition and wins, depression and let down overtook Michael as he struggled with weight gain, packing on 20 plus pounds.

He spent much of his recent 2 years improving his understanding of himself and his world and has, as a result, become a better man in the process.

The role of a healthy brain plays an important part in optimizing an individual's entire existence. Through a person's brain they view and understand their world. The human brain provides much of the content for personality, character, judgment and ability to make good choices. When the brain is working, a person is healthy. However, when the brain vitality is in trouble, there is a diminished ability in all areas of life.

Miraculous healing 'Brain Protocols' are quite possibly the most powerful of all the healings we are able to provide working through the human blueprint. The brain with all its amazing complexities, when restored to great function, can improve virtually all conditions of malfunction in the body.

The brain controls all the systems of the physical body and even some parts of the energetic body. For people in pain, healing the brain can restore the nerves to ease and equilibrium resulting in reduced or a total clearing of pain. Digestion is also affected positively by restoring the brain to a healthy state. When the brain colors are improved, chemistry can be improved through energy healings.

My research on the brain began many years ago, as I have also experienced depression and attention deficit related to a traumatic brain injury. What I have discovered in my research is that if you heal the brain, even post-traumatic stress disappears as the new brain cells and brain patterns literally erase the PTSD from the field of memory.

Improving the quality of a person's life with attention deficit can be done by clearing the five brains of grey and black energetic colors and by addressing the level of how the individual handles the amount of information flowing in from the extra pathways found in ADHD and ADD folks.

Depression is addressed in a similar fashion; however, the focus after clearing colors is to improve chemistry, often working with the hypothalamus and pituitary gland. We are using Cellular Neo Genesis ® which is the actual regeneration of a master stem cell in the area being improved.

# MALE LEADERS:
# BRAiN SECRETS UNCOvERED!

In my many years of brain regeneration with top leaders in all walks of life I have had the privilege and pleasure of working with the greatest minds of this age. I have improved the function of brains for scientists working at NASA and Stanford, Silicon Valley tech virtuosos as well as leaders in the Pentagon and human potentials field.

Working with the Quantum Field I have developed the tools and techniques for accessing the stem cells from the perfected human blueprint, brought them to 100% and started a cascade of new cell growth refreshing the regenerated brain to a set point of 100%. This process dramatically improves brain capacity and function for men and women of all ages.

Men tend to 'own' their logical and survival brain better then women. These are the brains involved with running an empire, protecting the tribe and creating order to the projects. Women tend to have a stronger hold on their emotional and creative brains. This supports nurturing and bonding as well as a natural calming and connecting influence with groups.

How well men and women use their five brains (survival, emotional, creative, logical and genius) is sourced and supported by the hormones the brain was marinated in as it developed. Little boys experienced large doses of testosterone and proceeded to make crashing noises, jump around and conquer their world even as toddlers while the estrogen driven female brain would nurture her dolls, entertain her stuffed animals with tea parties and as she progressed into tweendom—clothes shopping.

Left unregenerated the male and female brain will function as it was designed from the cavemen era with instinct driving the brain responses.

As we enter a new age and era, we are in a rectifying stage of human development. Women are holding leadership roles. Men are nurturing and caring for the young. The best of leadership for men is to integrate the creative and some of the emotions that strengthen trust and confidence from their followers. For women, the stronger activations of the logical and survival brains will help them focus and follow through, helping them to take positions of greater influence and reach.

Women, as we see in the brain study have less hold on their logical brain, while men less ability in the emotional and creative brains.

Brain one survival, brain two emotional, brain three creative, brain four logical and brain five genius.

| Gender & Age | Average of Brain 1 | Average of Brain 2 | Average of Brain 3 | Average of Brain 4 | Average of Brain 5 |
|---|---|---|---|---|---|
| Female | 23 | 36 | 32 | 27 | 12 |
| Gen Y | 23 | 34 | 20 | 23 | 11 |
| Gen X | 23 | 36 | 33 | 27 | 12 |
| Baby Boomers | 23 | 36 | 32 | 27 | 12 |
| Silent Generation | 15 | 16 | 33 | 34 | 7 |
| Male | 26 | 31 | 36 | 41 | 12 |
| Gen Y | 17 | 22 | 23 | 15 | 8 |
| Gen X | 26 | 28 | 29 | 43 | 13 |
| Baby Boomers | 27 | 33 | 38 | 41 | 13 |
| Silent Generation | 23 | 21 | 43 | 49 | 10 |

By Gender (with Generation Breakdown in some cases)

Silent Generation 1920–1944
Baby Boomers 1944–1964
Gen Y 1964–1984
Gen X 1984–2004

As we move father away from the Piscean patriarchal age we see the toppling of organizations whose structure and development relied entirely on 'man' power. The reference of a 'good old boys club' is no longer a good club to be identified with. It reflects a separatist, better then others click, no longer valued in society. Actually that club is disappearing as well-educated experienced men and women take their places in leadership in both corporations and entrepreneurial roles. We see an increase of loving creative male leaders welcoming their sisters into collaborative leadership roles with open arms!

Are you ready to experience the Only Brain Regeneration program in the world using the Quantum Field?

# MODULE TWO:
# THREE SECRETS OF MIRACULOUS HEALINGS AND BUILDING NEWCELLS

# DETOXiFY AND CLEAR:
# PUMP YOUR WAY TO FREEDOM

The number one thing I do with my students is clear them. Yes its true, even before regeneration the most important process creating a firm foundation for health wealth love and great success is to clear.

## Where the Problems Originate

The number one area where harmful programs lurk is in the supporting realm of amplification. It is in this field or realm that we find soul contracts, demonic, satanic and evil spirit curses and unfortunately spiritual parasites.

The field of amplification is our law of attraction accelerator. But if you are a person who loves to watch television shows that show murders, war movies, or bang—bang shoot 'em up movies, your field is rapidly acquiring information you likely don't want in your field.

Group mind is also notorious for adding problems that limit your joy and full self-expression, and this can move into family program in DNA and bloodline/clan challenges.

Together you and I clear all the parts of the human blueprint and get you pumping your way to freedom and full self-expression with a happier healthier body.

Getting the exact knowledge and understanding of what you are clearing and how to progress through a clearing is vital to 100% success.

## Core Life Challenges

I recently spent 100 hours clearing betrayal. Wow you say that sounds crazy, right? Not really. Think about collecting harmful programs an entire lifetime. And then amplify that by many lifetimes you have experienced and finally add to that your family influence. There's a whole heck of a lot in programs and thought forms causing you to show up as who you are.

What are your core issues? What have you been challenged with your entire life?

Betrayal

Emotional and Physical Toxicity

Servitude

Lack of Self Love

Violence and Abuse

Take a minute to listen to the voices in your head... yep I am actually telling you this once to listen to them, they are keeping your core challenges strong. When you learn to clear the core challenges you also at the same time clear the voices who would keep those negative looping thoughts going for a lifetime.

Once clear we can move to sustain and nurture. This is the area where rebuilding your life, whether new cells are needed or a new field for wealth and abundance are called for. And the final step in quantum activations is the amplification and acceleration of all good. In this phase you can reach your highest expression of self and really step into a powerful life of joy, love and yes, contribution to others.

So let's focus on getting you clear and detoxified. This is where the real movement happens when beginning your journey of quantum rejuvenation.

# SPiRiTUAL PARASiTES AND PESTS

If you have ever had a migraine, you know it hurts. It has 'crazy' symptoms; flicking, blurred or poor vision, stabbing in parts of the brain, extreme light and sound sensitively, nausea, weakness to name a few. Doctors are ready and willing to prescribe the latest in migraine control medication, but are at a loss as to why this happens.

Some link the phenomenon to changing chemistry and stress, and I fully agree to these notions but the actual pain, and suffering comes from the spiritual parasites and pests, Jesus way back in his day was casting out and helping people to return to themselves.

## Casting Out Demons

Mark 16:9
When Jesus rose early on the first day of the week, he appeared first to Mary Magdalene, out of whom he had driven seven demons.

Matthew 8:16
That evening many demon-possessed people were brought to Jesus. He cast out the evil spirits with a simple command.

John 14: 12

Very truly I tell you, whoever believes in me will do the works I have been doing, and they will do even greater things than these, because I am going to the Father.

## Jewish Concepts

Demons live in deserts or ruins (Lev. 16:10; Isa. 13:21; 34:14). They inflict sickness on men (Ps. 91:5–6). They trouble men's minds (Saul; I Sam. 16:15, 23) and deceive them (I Kings 22:22–23)

## From Hinduism

Rakshasas were created from the breath of Brahma when he was asleep at the end of the Satya Yuga. As soon as they were created, they were so filled with bloodlust that they started eating Brahma himself. Brahma shouted "Rakshama!" (Sanskrit for "protect me!") and Vishnu came to his aid, banishing to Earth all Rakshasas (thus named after Brahma's cry for help).

In each of these situations, a person will say about themselves: "I am not myself," "I feel overtaken," "it's weird I am not moving my legs something else is doing it." The panic comes over me all at once for no reason, I feel I can't catch my breath."

WEIRD is a good word to signal this is an invasion of a sort and with help you can once and for all free yourself from the troubling energy invaders who are at fault for your   problems.

With each of these three issues I want to encourage you to develop some healthy habits that will help you won your body more, and have less of this 'stuff' show up.

Step one is to follow a guided meditation daily that has you clear and own the power centers of the body, as well as getting your spirit fully filling out your physical body. An excellent choice from my many meditations is Dynamism. Understand that you've had unwelcome guests your entire life, and now it's time to really take charge and have you take back your body. They've   gotten used to being there. Think of them as squatters—they've got to be kicked out and then you need to own the spaces they've hung out in.

Step two: "This is Not ME" Affirm this anytime you feel a sudden onset of pain, anxiety or irregular movement in the body that you did not originate. This is a subtle distinction and it is difficult at first to get, but once you really get, we'll be on the same page together and you'll be in better shape.

Allow me to explain: when you say I have a migraine, you have now owned it by saying "I have." This is giving full permission for the causer of the pain to stay and continue to run the cycle of pain. When you say I am experiencing pressure or strong pressure n my head but this is not me my brain is relaxed and vibrant every minute of the day, you have done something very powerful. You have now said I feel it but it is not me, I don't believe it has to be there; my natural state is always peace and vibrancy.

Let me give you an example, I was lifting weights and in a dance move I threw my right shoulder holding a weight up in the air and I heard it pop. Okay now my previous belief would have been I have caused pain, or I am in pain. The belief in pain would have brought spiritual parasites to the site, to increase and prolong the pain, possibly for weeks. But this time I said, that's not me my shoulder feels great all the time, for 5 minutes. And guess what? No pain, my shoulder quickly returned to normal.

Step three: Let nature help you heal. The aura can develop holes and tears from which unwanted spiritual parasites can enter and have access to you, walking in nature, can begin to help the aura in its natural healing process. It can also dramatically improve body chemistry and what I know is when hormones or neurotransmitters are off, you are more susceptible to and invasion. Think about the poor gals who suffer from PMS. I've heard them describe themselves as feeling like a Sniper... definitely not the woman in charge but an overtaking of her body as hormones shift. So get out in nature!

The path to full body ownership and a body free of pain is a combination of detoxing or clearing and nurturing and getting life in balance. The biggest detox you can experience is the 7-hour freedom from spiritual parasites and pest program.

# SEvEN FUNDAMENTALS FOR LiviNG AN EXTRAORDiNARY LiFE

Living into your 100% life means living an exemplary life. You will become the guiding light to your friends and followers as you show the well-lit path towards the ever-unfolding magnificent existence. You choose.

I am often asked how I am able to live such a rich and full life, through the intense illness and the ups and downs mentally and emotionally from having multiple cancers and 17 surgeries. Along the way of 100% health I've discovered the secret path to living an extraordinary life. Your existence is not defined by the complicated set of circumstances life brings you.

Rather, living an extraordinary life is a conscious choice to be and become your greatness.

I have discovered seven fundamental elements of life that when engaged to the fullest expression will result in 100% human fulfillment. This is your guide to life well lived.

### 1. vitality - Having a Great Cellular Constitution

Your vitality and energetic presence give you the winning edge. When you are healthy, people around you feel safe and confident. More than that, you feel unstoppable. You are able to make plans and follow through with great velocity and intention. Enjoying a healthy body is the most important element, as it creates the ground from which you can soar. Without good health you live a life pieced together, built on a shaky foundation.

### 2. Alignment and Purpose

Alignment with your spiritual journey and connection with source is the second element of living an extraordinary life. To be in alignment will require you to take time away from the hustle and bustle of life and the pressures of group mind and family agreements. The greatest quest you can engage in is to discover who you are and what you are up to in this life. To live authentically, you must know who you are and why you are here. Making your best guess or operating on autopilot is not good enough. Make time for you to know yourself.

### 3. Discipline to Strength

A person who knows discipline is able to fulfill their mission and gain the respect of all those who they come in contact with. Discipline is the path to fulfillment of everything made manifest. To be healthy, wealthy and wise you must engage in a strategic discipline. Personal power comes from the ability to follow through. You can only experience discipline when you have cleared the entire muddle and 'squirrels'/distractions from your path. You must first fuel yourself, meaning you must fill yourself up to emotional fulfillment. When you are filled up you have a greater capacity to be emotionally generous with yourself and all others.

## 4. Enthusiasm for Truth

When you blend enthusiasm with truth you open to your greatest expression of self. As you enthusiastically call truth to you, you continue your journey towards awakening to your divine nature and powerful access to miraculous energies. Enthusiasm lights the way to higher wisdom. The one caveat to this conversation is to not get caught up with your version of truth. When truth has an opinion, it is actually a belief rather than an absolute. Truth has no other version. It just is.

## 5. Ascension the Progress of Your Awakening

The journey of ascension does not require you to consciously drive towards spiritual awakening. In this case your balanced loving life will move you towards your ascension. I now see the opportunity for full enlightenment, which includes mastery in the spiritual realm as well as the emotional, mental and physical realms. It is a deeper, richer type of enlightenment then just a spiritual awakening. The old awakening model was to throw all your intention into a spiritual journey and remove yourself from the world so as to gain enlightenment. This is still a valid journey, but a higher enlightenment of the human experience is the mastery of all aspects of your life, leaving nothing behind.

## 6. Mindset—Love-magic—Love-wisdom

To have your mind in the right place makes all the difference in living an extraordinary life. Having the brain working well with all the neurotransmitters and chemistry supporting your joyous bliss-filled life is a vital part of your successful experience. When you are in love with your life and with all those who you interact with, you have mastered your mindset and your life. Remember a healthy brain gives you the ground for healthy emotions. The awareness of the oneness of all things is the mystery and the doorway to glory.

## 7. Connection - Love Appreciation

This leads us into the final element and the bookend that holds this magnificent formula together. Appreciation for everything and everyone is the greatest lesson and expression of human kind. Love is always the answer. If your days are filled with gratitude and appreciation for the wonderful life you are now living, even if some days are not so wonderful, staying with the grace of appreciation will install the deepest connection to the Divine and to the great majesty and wonder of humankind.

Living into your 100% life means living an exemplary life. You will become the guiding light to your friends and followers as you show the well-lit path towards the ever-unfolding magnificent existence. You choose. Know that you have always had the opportunity to choose. Now I invite you to consciously make a choice for greatness. Join me in living an extraordinary life, and be filled with the peace and bliss that surpasses thought or mental understanding. Be.

# WE MUST TEACH CHiLDREN SPiRiTUAL HYGiENE OR THEY FACE EARLY iLLNESS AND DEATH

## American Spiritual Crisis Point

Children are not being taught how to care for their spiritual body. As a result they grow up with no spiritual hygiene tools and become sick—physically, emotionally, mentally and spiritually. This results in illness in all areas of the human experience. Some die early, all because they lack the awareness of authentic internal self-care.

Researches for the 'cure' movements tell us we must fight cancer, MS, heart disease, etc., and promote the fund-raising organizations with our support. We are told that they are promoting the idea that their research gives individuals who are suffering more birthdays.

It is possible, if we were promoting a wellness and spiritual cleanliness, individuals would live hundreds of years and circumvent illness advancing to any serious concerns or life- threatening circumstances.

In reality, the fund-raising promotions are reactive. They are not promoting an authentic movement for positive health and longevity. Keep in mind the treatments that these research organizations promote; they actually kill the health of both the sick and the healthy cells. There is no method of restoring health to the cellular and energetic body. Individuals going through the treatments may live longer than they would have had they not had the treatments; however, the body loses light, vitality and life force from these treatments.

What is the answer to this dilemma?

How can we move out of a reactive health protocol to an authentic wellness lifestyle?

Children and adults need to be educated. Humans are all radiant beings of light, with an innate ability to heal, born with a miraculous system and directly connected to the divine.

Spiritual shower in a simple daily meditation clears the aura, chakras, meridians and seat of the soul. It energizes and restores the systems to health and vitality, daily. Practicing this style of meditation allows the individual to be in charge of their health and longevity.

When the body breaks down, e.g., a child gets a cold, the parent or the child can improve the energy of the body and the cells. Being able to use a simple technique to identify the low energy systems and areas of the body and then tuning up these areas with gold energy can often end the illness immediately, while other times it allows the process of healing to speed up.

Let go of group mind (memes) when it comes to illness, disease and death. Human beings are radiant beings of light with bodies meant to live hundreds of years.

# CAN YOU MAKE A MiRACLE?

## The Miraculous Legacy of Our Lady of Lourdes

The three Secrets to creating Miracles revealed. Remembering the Blessed Mother's Appearances in 1858 and the importance of Love!

Miracles in Modern Times—Our Lady of Lourdes Celebrated in February Every Year

February 11, 1858 is the historic day Catholics set aside to remember the miraculous appearances of Mother Mary in Lourdes France to a school girl in the city dump. From the communications between the Blessed Virgin and young Bernadette Soubirous; love, hope and devotion sprung up in a dark and hopeless period. Faith suddenly was renewed. The sick and down-hearted flocked to the small village in France to experience the miraculous appearances and healing waters. The miracle producing water generated in the last visitation are to present day are drawn on for the hope of a miraculous cure when medicine can offer none.

## Three Secrets to Creating Miracles Today

1. Faith ~ Know in your heart it is possible
2. Frequency of Unconditional Love or higher for the generation of a positive life changing miracle
3. Connection ~ Accessing the power of Creation

Historical accounts of the appearances of Mother Mary suggest that only one individual visually saw the Blessed Lady. Young visionary Bernadette, 14-year-old daughter to an unemployed father who had previously enjoyed work as a miller and her mother an over worked stressed out washer woman. This family lived in the worst of homes: an old prison room that was prone to flooding during the rainy season.

The experience of devotion and mystery, the compelling interactions of rapture lend credibility to the story of Bernadette and the Lady, yet when the actual miracles began there was no doubt amongst believers that this was a real and divine experience.

Miraculous apparitions of Mary, Jesus, Angels and Holy Ones reach deep through historic legend over the past 2,000 years since the Avatars Mary and Jesus appeared and lived among us. Their mission; to provide us with a road map, the blueprint for a life that if emulated would allow each and every one of us to create a miraculous life.

Jesus said; 'What so ever I have done my friend, this and much more you shall also do.' He taught us to follow the path of prayer and meditation, to study and to embody compassion. In his last hours in the garden of Gethsemane he showed us one more time how to commune with the Divine.

Charity (generosity) and the vibration of pure unconditional love are excellent vibrations to begin in the creation of an extraordinary shift and ultimately a miracle.

The Agape Love of Jesus and Mary Jesus came to introduce humanity to the new realm of love and freedom. His message is one of love.

'Beloved let us love one another, for love is of God and everyone that loveth is born of God and knoweth God, He that loveth not knoweth not God for God is Love Beloved let us love one another.' 1 John 4:7–8

Love one another as I have loved you.

The Love Wisdom Creed from the new rosary 'Illumination'

There is one infinite God/ Goddess vibration of love that creates everything seen and unseen. This all prevailing presence is light, love, miraculous creation, and the sacred expression of inclusion. Divine love embraces all humanity, regardless of religious preference or any other human selective difference. Heaven is here on earth.

I am free to live a life of spiritual freedom and full self-expression liberated in love, gratitude and mastery in this body here and now. My spirit is limitless. I am responsible for any limits I experience in this body and have complete access to the divine through prayer and contemplation to release myself from any human bonds I have worn as spiritual clothing that no longer resonate with my essence.

I enjoy direct mystical access and divine union while practicing spiritual rites. These sacred rites belong to all humanity. In the Christian tradition they are known as Baptism, Rebirth, the Communion of Saints, the Sacrament of Communion and the Mystical Bridal Chamber. I follow the sacred path towards Spiritual Awakening, Enlightenment, Transmutation and Ascension in this life.

I experience the presence of the Christed one known to me as Jesus the Christ. Jesus Christ was Avatar, Teacher, Guide and friend. I revere blessed Mother Mary, who is compassion, love, forgiveness and healing. I trust in the existence of Holy Spirit who is essence living in me as life force.

I trust in the reality of the Holy Ones, the Divine Male and Female Deities who have sprung forth from all the great and lesser known spiritual paths to teach and guide us on the path of Love Wisdom.

I am ageless and timeless. My life continues in or out of this human temple I call my body. Whatever I have done willingly or unknowingly to myself or others that does not resonate with pure truth can be washed from me through the power of forgiveness and the unending limitless power of LOVE.

# TAKiNG RESPONSiBiLiTY FOR YOUR HAPPiNESS AND CLARiTY

It is entirely your responsibility to keep your spiritual, emotional, mental and physical bodies healthy, happy and clear.

What does it mean to be fully responsible for how life shows up? This is an amazing and eye opening concept. As you look at where you experience areas of breakdown or vibrancy in all aspects of your life, take note on where you live in your ownership of that area.

Look at the areas in your life that are happy and clear. What are the common denominators that make these parts of your life so stellar? Here are some possible answers:

- Grounded
- You work it
- Regular practice
- You have support in place to be successful
- You really like it
- You identify it as a great part of yourself
- It's a natural part of you
- You go to it in your mind to fortify yourself when you need a boost

If you stumble on your path you have choice to ask for assistance, but no one owes you your wellness.

You create vibrancy and joy in all aspects of your life by good choices every moment.

Grab a pen and paper and write down all the areas in your life that are not working. Let your mind relax and think about who you have assigned responsibility to for these areas. Imagine taking responsibility back.

Once you have taken responsibility for these scattered pieces of yourself, make a clean, fresh list of these situations. Under each item write down three things that would increase your happiness and ownership of each area. It's time to get actively involved with your fully embodied passionate life.

# HOW THE BiG MiRACLE COMES TRUE FOR WHALES AND HUMANS

The Big Miracle, real life magic afoot with Whales and Humans

Hear the story of Carolyn Stevens, former Dominican Sister, about her transformation from death to life..."I feel like Lazareth, raised from the dead."

The story of 'The Big Miracle' currently in theaters tells the true-life saga of three huge grey whales and their struggle to survive the life and death nature of their predicament. Carolyn Stevens' journey is the story of a wife and mother, her struggle to survive a terminal illness, staying alive and raising her daughter.

Her story includes the devotion of her family and the need to create a miracle and save her life.

When we begin the journey of what makes a miracle, we must first look to its very definition…

In both the case of the whale family and the human family there was little to no hope of survival.

The whales, Fred, Wilma and Bam Bam, a family of three, were held brutally captive. They were trapped with virtually no chance of making it out of the frozen ice prison. Their miracle would require escaping death and swimming to open seas, for migration to warmer, friendlier waters.

Carolyn was told by her doctors that there wasn't any hope. Facing no additional medical intervention, she was preparing to die. Her miracle would require full body regeneration.

Was it a miracle that humans, with opposing and divergent interests, came together in a battle to save the whales despite their adamant and hostile differences? The real life story unfolds with amazing twists and turns. Healing, love, acceptance and focused passionate movement to save the family of helpless giants becomes the mission for opposing sides. What we see on the big screen is evidence of humanity. The human spirit emerges in Technicolor as the whales find their way to freedom, thanks to the efforts of; the Inuit peoples, the National Guard, President Reagan, State government, Green Peace, the media, the Russian Military, private industry and group-mind energy of all the school children across the country.

When I think of this epic shift, I think of the old song from the 60s:

"One man's hands can't tear a prison down,
two man's hands can't tear a prison down,
but if two and two and fifty make a million,
we'll seethat daycomeround, we'll seethat daycomeround!"

The baby whale, Bam Bam, had not the strength or health to survive the torturous ordeal, but Fred and Wilma made their escape, through amazing and courageous human effort.

Carolyn's saga is also full of twists and turns; as her friend Bill watches her passing away, he reaches out to a miraculous healer and pleads with her to call The Stevens to begin the healing process.

## A Dramatic Shift

A dramatic shift happens with Carolyn, on her first visit to Miraculous Healer Julie Renee. The death energy from the core of her body is removed. Literally, 18 inches of spiritually black energy is lifted from Mrs. Stevens in the first encounter. With daughter Chrissy and husband Charles present, they watch with desperate hope that some miracle will save Carolyn. Over the next few weeks Charles and Carolyn coordinate the healing efforts of Julie Renee with the medical professionals, who had been treating and prescribing. In truly short order, Carolyn was returning to her life, weaning off the heavy medication schedule. Carolyn began to get her life back. As seven deadly infections were removed from her body, a spiritually blessed life returned. (Carolyn is later successful in having the reattachment procedure.)

"I believe at the core of a miracle, is the strong belief, that a miracle is possible." The Green Peace character, Drew Barrymore played, declared that the miracle would happen, period.

Carolyn and Charles who themselves are devote Catholics knew that a miracle could happen for them, with absolute certainty.

Carolyn's background as a Catholic sister and a university professor had her marrying her husband later in life. The blessings of a daughter in their life kept them young, and the desire, on my part, to keep this family together was unquestionable. I knew deeply and profoundly, to my core, that I would not let Carolyn leave behind the family she so loved and deserved. With the help of the divine, we would create together the miracle of new health and life restored.

A miracle requires certainty; it requires love–powerful unending love, and the hand of the divine. We are all radiant Beings of Light, with an innate ability to heal, to love and make manifest the glory of God every day of our lives. Have you asked for a miracle lately? If not… perhaps it is time to remember, that you are a beloved child of God. You are wanted and needed in this blessed Garden of Eden.

# 11% OF AMERiCANS SUFFER FROM A CLiNiCAL "FiNANCiAL" DEPRESSiON: FiNDiNG OUR WAY BACK

11% of Americans Adults are Currently Using Anti-Depressants. Do Finances Have You Down? Severe crisis in the heart and minds of the American people, is it time to return to living an authentic life, from the inside out?

The problem today is that people throughout the United States have become depressed and hopeless. They no longer believe that they have an innate ability to create wealth. Our country built on financial freedom is now in a mental/emotional collapse.

Shockingly, 11% of Americans are on antidepressants.

Five-year-old children entering kindergarten are now experiencing stress levels of 9th graders. The constant barrage of news reels speaks of how badly broken we are and how corrupt governmental systems are that could fix the problems. There is apparently no hope for recovery.

Fear and depression have caused a communal amnesia (Meme). Somehow we have forgotten the fact that all humans are radiant beings of light. This concept has become a phantom memory. Americans no longer remember that they are children of the divine and are living in the Garden of Eden.

"My God when I open my eyes and look around I have forgotten all you've given me. My heart is over flowing and my eyes are filled with tears," (Suddhi Bisa Ragai, Bengali Poetry). Featured song (sung in Bengali) on the music CD, Gratitude, Recording artist Julie Renee. Contact us for details on all of Julie Renee's Music CD's Info@julierenee.com

Here are four steps for moving out of financial depression and into a life of radiant, authentic wealth.

1. Turn off violent and depressing programming on TV. Take a break from the news and start living. Put importance on relationships and all your good fortune.
2. Decide on what you want to create now. You must positively make a choice and then bring your will and mental force forward to create movement out of a stagnant condition.
3. Get into present-time and let go of what has fallen away or failed. Put the past in the past and reinvent your wonderful, new present-time life.
4. Believe that it is possible for you to have your wonderful life here and now. Remember how powerful the mind is; what the mind conceives and believes, it will achieve.

The fact that 11% of the American population is currently on antidepressants represents a country in real emotional crisis. It is time to slow down and return to a life lived from the inside out. True wealth isn't about ownership or dollars in the bank. Authentic wealth starts with loving yourself and your life, enjoying good health and good relationships and finally a life with the riches that support you and your beautiful life.

# FOR A GREAT MOOD
# GET OUTDOORS

Peoplewhoexercisejustfiveminutesadayoutdoorsimprovetheir moodandreducethenegativeimpactsofstress(especiallywhen the outdoor activity is close to a natural water source).
—From a University of Essex Study

For years I have been singing to the tune of outdoor meditation reflection and exercise as the healing balm for just about all that ails the human being. With a rich hike in the mountains you can literally reboot your brain, and rebalance your negative and positive ions. The natural world is a place to return to your authentic self and re-emerge from a difficult passage.

## Three Tips for Reaping the Highest Benefits From Nature

1. Schedule time to enjoy the out of doors. Camping, hiking, jogging, swimming, and even canoeing or kayaking don't just happen in an active schedule. Make it a priority, and prepare with great hiking shoes, water to hydrate and a great attitude.

2. Go into nature with gratitude and celebration in your heart and mind. Noticing all the glories of nature and praising source every moment for the great goodness you have received in this amazing planet is the trick to a magnetic personality.

3. Breathe deeply. When you are out in nature, practice the art of breathing. It matters not if you are an expert at pranic breathe, or you use some techniques used to get you through early stages of labor, altering breath patterns can restore the brain, and improve circulation and muscle health.

# MODULE THREE: DNA AND STEM CELL REGENERATION

# QUANTUM REJUvENATiON AND STEM CELLS: THE REAL STORY

Stem cells are a truly amazing gift in your human design! What we've discovered in our research on Master Cells (a special kind of stem cell) is the key to growing healthy and ultimately growing younger. By using stem cells activated and regenerated with the quantum field allows us to literally grow back a surgically removed organ or gland.

## Stem Cell

A cell that upon division replaces its own numbers and also gives rise to cells that differentiate further into one or more specialized types, as various B cells and T cells.

In a recent conversation with my friend Jerry Crabtree genetic scientist at Stanford was that the scientists are working on the same things we are, just in a slow moving lab, with a 'prolonged' under the microscope review. Professor Crabtree's laboratory is currently researching skin cells, stem cells and healing the nerves. His projection is it may take 20 years to bring this project to a successful result. What they are doing is turning skin cells into nerve cells. One of the possible positive uses of this research is to rebuild a nervous system for someone who has Parkinson's disease.

This is a very exciting time in the field of genetic research, and parallels the Quantum research we are doing here. The Crabtree labs estimate 18 to 20 years of research and development prior to taking this extraordinary research out into the world to help folks.

With our stem cell regeneration techniques we are seeing glands and organs being rebuilt, restored and regenerated and we are getting anecdotal* medical documentation. (*meaning we are not a lab nor do we have the funding to do 20 years of research yetourparticipantshavemedicalreportsthatshowunexplainable miraculous results).

In my vision of the Human Blueprint and the role of the master cell is key to everything else related to health, happiness and rejuvenation.

—Julie Renee

Let's talk about what stem cells are and why they are so precious to us in the regeneration process. A stem cell by definition is an undifferentiated cell of a multicellular organism that is capable of giving rise to indefinitely more cells of the same type, and from which certain other kinds of cells arise by differentiation. Ok, so that's what the dictionary tells us. This is the intelligent cell that virtually holds the secret to building new cells. For me it is the most beautiful gift from the human blueprint! Stem cells and master stem cells are cells that hold the regeneration information it is their mission and purpose to restore and regenerate the body.

As my Apprentices and I look to the poor functioning gland, organ or system we observe stem cells at a very reduced rate of function. As I analyze these cells they may have a nucleus functioning at a very low percentile. For example, 11% and to make matters worse organelles for example an absorption organelle (kind of like the stomach of the cell) may also read very low function. Perhaps the DNA itself may be damaged or broken and the interior and exterior of the cell may be struggling. Imagine a poorly functioning cell that is supposed to help you grow healthy. Can you envision what it will reproduce in such a poor condition?

By all components of the cell using the quantum field and the perfect human blueprint to their 100% state, regeneration can now effectively and efficiently commence.

I'd like you to think about your Divine Human Blueprint as the spiritual model of your physical being. Since it is the blueprint, it is the 100% perfected version of you. The stem cells then, in this model are the very best version of yourself. Even when working with newborns, I see the stem cells are not at 100%. Activating the stem cell blueprint with the quantum field can transform everything.

Another way to imagine the human blueprint is to think of kirlian photography and a torn leaf. The area where the leaf was torn away still appears in the image. Also think of those who have lost a limb, yet they continue to have sensations and pain where the limb was. It was because the limb is still there on the level of essence.

# RECESSiVE DNAOBLiTERATiON

DNA programs are an amazing gift in the human blueprint. From DNA direction and instruction we humans are able to enjoy life. The unending miracles that are generated from this tiny complex central program give us all cause for celebration.

The core DNA structure is phenomenal. What we address in this protocol is the small three percent of DNA programs that do not serve our overall wellness and sense of health vitality, wealth and connection.

To clarify, this process is meant to give access to correcting the wiring that is causing your system to malfunction and be less available to your life in full self-expression. We will not in this process address how to correct or improve congenital or birth defects. We will focus on the improvement and correction of programs that cause illness, poor health, wealth and love issues.

Many of the new thought leaders are now speaking of the possibility of reprogramming DNA. I love that this has become a consciousness among the new and spiritual thinkers. What my intention is with this paper is to provide the real life black and white blueprint of how to permanently and fully alter the DNA that is causing you challenges.

Altering DNA starts with awareness that there is a recurring challenge whether it is a repetitive problem in your life or in your family history. You cannot, however, deeply alter your DNA through your mental body or by just thinking about it.

## Who Can Benefit From Recessive DNA Obliteration?

List of DNA Obliteration I have assisted with:

- Removal of Cancer Gene and Replacement of Healthy Cells (Breast Cancer)
- Removal of Mental Illness program, adding a program of vibrant stability and mental wellness.
- Removal of criminal activities, this DNA program runs in many amazing leaders who once cleared experience a rare and relieving freedom to sync up with their own full self-expression.
- Poor organ or gland function, and a restoration of health function (this typically will require several types of healing including cellular neo genesis to bring the body to full wellness. without clearing the DNA program all the other processes will eventually revert to the DNA program, months or years out. This is a necessary process for permanent wellness.
- Brain function malfunction to brain wellness. Great progress has been made in understanding Alzheimer's and Dementia as well as Attention Deficit Disorder. The DNA process done early enough can completely change how the challenge or health of the brain plays out.
- Love and relationship challenges are imprinted in DNA and can dramatically improve an individual's experience

of love and connection if the DNA landscape is especially troubling.
- Wealth and Abundance programs can either prevent full realization of the dream of full self-expression or when cleared create the freedom to soar.

These are several of the common recessive DNA upgrades I have routinely improved. Deep DNA alterations should only been carried out by a wise elder who understands the impact of the shifts on the person growth process and how their life will play out. A healer should never alter DNA without the go ahead from their divine connection and the permission of the person getting healed.

## Warning

Do not under any circumstances think you have permission because they are a family member, close friend or spouse. You will create potential problems for the person you are healing, and more importantly for yourself. Your life force can deplete, you can take on their health problems and karma (problems they brought in to grow as a human spirit, these are not the challenges you came in to deal with).

## Altering DNA impact

For many individuals the gift you give them by altering the recessive DNA programs will mean the difference between health and vitality or illness suffering and early death. For others it will allow them to embody the life they have carefully studied and trained for but have been unable to realize to this point because the cellular body is programmed from less them desirable direction.

Case studies one and two:
In the same year I worked with a well loved and respected Pilates instructor going through radical treatment for breast cancer

I was approached by a Scottish born artist whose mother had died of breast cancer who had a knowing it was just around the corner for her. We care for each individual based on their possibility for wellness and honor their limitations.

The Pilates instructor chose hands on healing and some intuitive guidance and, although I offered her the advanced deeper healing, she felt her path, which was of extreme suffering with chemo therapy was her choice. I watched her literally become a walking skeleton as she could not hold food down. I was able to help her visualize colors that calmed the body, but her need to direct the movement of recovery and inability to step into the next level of wellness dominated her mindset. We did stop working together. The last time I saw her she look like a twig, fragile and brittle, holding on for life in a barbaric system. Her doctor said she would likely not survive past the 5 year mark because of the type and stage of cancer she had.

The Scottish Artist was quite the opposite. She had not yet become ill and, though she was challenged with some significant health issues, she was open hearted and knew that a Recessive DNA process would give her a prolonged and happy life with her young son and husband. We were in one session able to remove the massive cancer programs in her DNA and reprogram the new life story with her authentic god health experience. Years later, happy health and glowing with a sense of ease and a long life ahead of her she experiences a kind of freedom and future anticipation she could not have held prior to the clearing process. Recent DNA test shows no cancer DNA!

### Case study three:

St. Louis event planner losing the use of her legs from neuropathy. With further research we discover most the generations before her several direct family members, like parents and grandparents, had their legs or feet amputated in later life. She was unable to feel her feet most of the time and had numbness running up her leg, especially above the right knee. I was new to DNA work back then, though our efforts to heal her were absolutely remarkable. She regained full feeling and use of her legs and was able to return to a normal active life in just four short months. We did regrow the nerves through cellular regeneration after the DNA program was obliterated and we removed a significant amount of unwanted 'information.'

She is happily living an active life, full use of legs and an amazing spirit living out her legacy in the world, able to fulfill her human spirit mission!

### Case study four:

Many years ago I discovered I could alter my DNA. I wondered why I was always having to diet and why it seemed like I was always fighting to maintain my youthful slender shape. As I investigated further I saw that both sides of the family DNA were programmed for significant weight gain after age 35. Since both sides of the family had servitude pictures, and poverty pictures in the DNA program, the family body program was to gain weight so one would have the capacity to survive a serious illness like scarlet fever or the plague. I was able to remove the recessive programming for weight gain and the slave pictures.

I have, since that time, consistently stayed under 139. I am 5'6" (previously had my weight climb up to 152) and have constantly maintained a six figure income, something I had only done 2 x's before.

When DNA changes your mindset, also naturally upgrades and you begin to explore a world, and a life out of the constraints you previously operated from.

You are a radiant being of light. You were meant to have this knowledge. For generations this knowledge has been hidden; what you might have naturally learned as a child is now being shown to you. Understand that there is a love wisdom culture that provides the space for unparalleled shifts and changes.

Recommended Reading: Your Divine Human Blueprint Recessive DNA Obliteration

# HOW TO CHANGE YOUR UNHEALTHY
# DNA WiTH THE QUANTUMFiELD

If you "Google" (change DNA—Deoxyribonnucleic acid, a self-replicating material present in nearly living organisms as the main constituent of chromosomes. It is the carrier of genetic information) you will find many articles out on how meditation helps improve your DNA. It's pretty exciting to know that the Human Blueprint is responsive to your good actions. You may have heard that it is now possible to change your DNA in a more directed and conscious way. New thought leaders have been talking about it for years. I remember attending a millionaire mind workshop with hundreds of people in attendance. T. Harv Eker was guiding us to use our thoughts to improve our situation… and I was thrilled so many people were really listening! Now a days there are a number of experts in the field of DNA shifting each having a unique name for their specific version of transformation but the process of altering DNA or what I call DNA Obliteration is a very doable and simple to follow procedure that yields incredible results.

## DNA

Deoxyribonucleic acid, a self-replicating material present in nearly all living organisms as the main constituent of chromosomes. It is the carrier of genetic information.

I began exploring DNA years ago in a spiritual wellness training program hosted by a spiritual institute in Northern California. In the 3 year training we were given the opportunity to fine tune our inner vision and to look closely at one of our own DNA strands.

When observing the DNA strand I began to see the flaws in it. I noticed strands had broken pieces—there were dark areas and although my vision of DNA was cartoonish in nature, I could see the beauty and the opportunity in gaining more awareness and knowledge of this part of my design.

Ironically this group wanted to keep the secrets for their students on observing and shifting the health of the body a philosophy I understand, but do not align with. In this case the elegant design of the blueprint is meant to be accessed and used to create a shift in health, vitality and a global awakening to what we were meant to become.    Imagine knowing how to improve your health and live hundreds of years...how much better we would be able to use our brains as  wise elders with tremendous capacity and love  wisdom.
—Julie Renee

I chose to research the programs in  my  DNA that seemed to always be asking my body to put on more fat than I was comfortable with in my belly, thighs and legs. I used a vacuum cleaner process (meaning I imagined a golden shop vac cleaning off my DNA and ridding it off these programs. I successfully removed the DNA responsible for the overproduction of fat on my belly and legs. While tuned in to my inner vision I had a unique experience of female family members who had   passed on showing up energetically in my space to intercede. With my inner vision I experienced their concern about tweaking this DNA. Since my family on both mother and fathers side had suffered from extreme poverty, the gene for extra fat and weight was considered important and necessary for survival. With the extra fat a woman would potentially survive typhoid fever or the plague. I reassured these family spirit guides that I was in good shape and this issue of needing excessive fat stores to survive illness would not be a consideration. I removed the fat DNA and have avoided putting on extra pounds all these many years.

That was my first experiment with DNA. It was exciting to see I could make an impact on my own body. Years later with a very developed and efficient technique for removal of unwanted DNA I have worked on removing cancer DNA and dementia and all other DNA related issues on a daily basis for my clients.

A popular subject I am asked to help with daily is the issue of poor money programming. Poverty or the ability to break the glass ceiling is often like weight. If the body is working against you it's hard to experience a lasting transformation. Removing poor money pictures includes, bringing in money, sustaining and growing wealth as well as raising your net worth. Bad money DNA can be removed. I did it for myself and you can also do it!

## One of Our Exciting Medical Miracles

One of our exciting medical miracles is from our dear friend Cecily Kate. She is a lovely woman from Scotland. Her mother, grandmother and aunt had died of breast cancer between age 45 and 65. Cecily Kate had gone to her doctor and the DNA test revealed she too would likely experience an early death to breast cancer. She had the cancer gene. She reached out to me after getting the medical report. She was very concerned as she had started her family later life she had hopes to live a long happy life. She wanted to see her son fill his destiny like all mothers wish. We removed the cancer DNA using the DNA Obliteration process found in my book Your Divine Human Blueprint, and upon re-checking her DNA, the doctors discovered she no longer had caner DNA in any of the cells of her body!

The message I got from her on my answering service was ecstatic to be given in a get out of jail card and freedom from breast cancer is a huge accomplishment. One I'm sure many women look for when they choose to undergo a double mastectomy to avoid breast cancer. I have known several women who have had this traumatic and mutilating procedure with the hopes to live with out cancer another day. Angelina Jolie was a celebrity who chose that route. I am sorry I did not know her personally to help her with this issue.

I have spelled out the exact steps of DNA Obliteration in my book and have devoted a chapter to furthering the understanding of this process and how each individual can on their own successfully remove harmful DNA from their body.

DNA removal is truly possible and is now a fact. Look to the current and near future to see revolutionary changes as people maintain their health for many years beyond what was originally patterned into them at birth. Alzheimer's will become obsolete and people will avoid terrible diseases like Parkinson's, muscular dystrophy and many, many other genetic abnormalities to live healthy, vibrant, strong, powerful lives.

Today is the Future, and you are alive to experience these powerful transformations now!

# HEALTHY DNA AND
# THE BREAST CANCER GENE

In this era of god knowledge and full self-expression there is an opening to take more control of your future, by improving your DNA and removing harmful genes that do not serve your happy healthy life.

There was a time when it was appropriate to have generations in a family experience the same illness. Perhaps your grandmother aunt and now you have diabetes. Maybe you're child has inherited a rare blood illness or perhaps like my client Kate, you have inherited the breast cancer gene, and are in line to become ill or even die at some point from this familial program. Well the great news is it just doesn't have to be that way anymore. All family genetics, and all illness genes can now be removed with a simple hand movement called the quantum pump.

What I've discovered in my research with breast cancer gene and all illness programs in the DNA for that matter is that it can permanently be removed from all the cells of your body... you can end the line of suffering, and not pass it along to future generations.

It was fun to work with Kate as she had gotten the medical test showing the markers, we worked together and removed it ad she went back getting a new DNA test with no cancer markers.

There's no need to have these tests, as kinesiology will verify both the presences and the absence of the gene, but it is nice to have the outer validation.

To learn about the full process of DNA Obliteration you'll find a step-by-step guide in Your Divine Human Blueprint, and I also train you in this technique thoroughly in the Online Diamond Immersion Training.

# MODULE FOUR:
# RESTORE BALANCE
# AND JOY TO YOUR LIFE

# NATiONAL FOOTBALL HERO
# JOE THEiSMANN SPEAKS
# ABOUT PROSTATE CHALLENGES

Now promoting natural, healthy prostate supplements; approaching men's health with common sense and natural solutions. Julie Renee addresses the problem Joe Theismann and so many men of maturing age face.

I was surprised to see my friend, football hero and Heisman trophy winner, Joe Theismann, on national TV promoting a solution for enlarged prostate and frequent urination issues interrupting his golf game. I am, however, glad that he has decided to take a transparent stand to encourage other healthy men to deal with the issue in a healthy, natural way.

Kudos, Joe, for using your fame for good, in what normally would be considered a taboo subject, at least for television. Joe is promoting what looks like a somewhat natural herbal formula, purchased without a prescription, to help prostate health.

With so many men of the baby boomer age reaching a time where this may be an issue, let's explore a few natural cures found in miraculous healings and meditations.

One of the problems with the prostate is that sitting and lack of use or energetic clearing can back up energy and cause problems, especially enlargement of the prostate.

In the newer meditations coming out of our Miraculous Living Sound Studio, we have not only included the healing and release of energy from the ovaries for women, but are clearing the testes and prostate for men. This is an especially wonderful technique for prevention of future problems.

What if you are already having problems and the prostate is enlarged or you are having the sudden and frequent urination urges? There are several things to do that dramatically improve the situation. These items can be addressed in either the private one-to-one healings with me or one of my certified miraculous healers, or in our miraculous healing weekends. Yes, we definitely address this very important issue in the group healings, where we often have more men than women in the room.

## Men's Health Healing Protocol

1. Discover the color and function of the prostate, testes, bladder and urethra. This is done using kinesiology. Typically the function will be very low and the color grey or black (energetically). The dark color will mean that it is in an unhealthy or death pattern and cannot regenerate into health at this point.

2. Pump gold energy into each of the 4 areas until color and function return to a healthy color.
   Best colors:
   Prostrate: cobalt blue 100%, orange 90%
   Testes: apple green 100%, yellow 98%, peacock blue 90%
   Bladder: pink 100%, yellow 93%
   Urethra: sky blue 100%, mint green 94%, red 83%

3. The process of shrinking any enlarged tissue (for women this works well with fibroids also) is to do the rose-bomb technique. Essentially you will imagine putting the image of a rose on the enlarged prostate to absorb the excess energy. Next, imagine a cartoon bomb exploding the rose, taking the energy with it, thus shrinking the energy holding the enlargement.

Although the herb saw palmetto is recommended for supporting prostrate health, I understand it takes a whole lot more herb then you can possibly ingest to provide significant improvement for the inconvenient condition of enlarged prostate.

Yogis have always practiced sublimating sexual energy with a meditation technique. While in meditation allow the sexual energy to rise up through the spine through the 6th chakra at the brow center, where it is comforted in the mental force and then out the top of the head. The energy problem is one of congestion in the male body, which just like backed up plumbing, will cause stress and strain on the system until something gives due to overload.

The fine art of keeping the body in balance and healthy at every age is our mission.

Please check out our website: www.julierenee.com to learn more.

# BLiSS AWARENESS

## instead of Stress Awareness Month ~ How About inner Bliss Awareness Month?

The nation honors the month of April each year as a year to be aware of stress and the devastating effects it can have on your life. You know me, always trying to turn lemons into DIAMONDS! (Forget lemonade, let's go for a transformation rather them just an upgrade.)

Stress can play an important and even a great role in your life if you know how to transform stress to positive actions, and times for reflection. Without stress we would all lolly-gag around turning into our own version of Jabba the Hutt. So how do we harness the positive powers of stress and allow the negative aspects to dissipate?

First off, understand if you are experiencing a negative stress, it may be that your mindset or point of view is not correctly attuned to the situation. Ask yourself, how am I looking at this? Is it a hardship? Is it draining? I promise you anything you are experiencing in a cumulatively negative way can also be experienced from a positive. Could you make a game of the situation? Could you give the task to another who enjoys it? What would need to shift in you to have fun in the  moment?

Next, look at how you plan your day and week. Write down everything that needs to be done and then create order for accomplishing everything over the next few weeks. When you leave everything up in your head there is a kind of intense urgent pressure that everything needs to be done urgently and right away. This is probably not the  truth.

Reevaluate; get it on a white board or a grid of some kind and begin to take the steps needed to succeed over time. Slow and steady does win the race and you can do it in grace and ease!

Finally, have you appreciated what you are stressed about? Is it giving you the next steps to your unfolding or showing you what needs to move to take your next big step up? Gratitude can shift a tremendous amount of tension and turn it into positive fuel for your unstoppable life!

# MODULE FivE:
# HEAL YOUR VISION

# viSiON

It's very exciting to realize that you can improve your vision without surgical procedures or vision enhancements, such as glasses, contacts or laser surgery. In my many years of healing work I have discovered how the visual system works and how to restore much of lost vision using several innovative and efficient procedures.

Your vision and the way you see the world can make a huge impact on your comprehension and understanding of life. Improving my own vision was my first experiment nine years ago. Having worn glasses for reading since age 18, I decided to access my regeneration abilities and strengthen my vision. This was before I really understood the divine human blueprint, and yet I was successful in reversing a vision condition that had been declining for 26 years. I created a strong intention, amplified by meditation and prayer, and over six months, my vision improved.

At the time, I was also struggling with a weakened immune system. I got to thinking that growing back my adenoids and tonsils might make a significant difference to my health and vitality, so, in meditation, I set a strong intention to grow them back.

When I went in for my annual vision test, my ophthalmologist was shocked. He declared, "Your vision has improved! That never happens in your age group." He concluded, "The results from the last exam must have been wrong." I assured him, no, the results were correct, and that by using my intention I had improved my vision. He shook his head, "It's not possible," he said. He checked to see who had done the last eye exam. "Puzzling," he said, "I did the exam."

A single restoration could easily be a fluke, but at my next medical visit my endocrinologist noticed that not only did I have tonsils, but they were also full-grown. He said, "They must have been there all along." I assured him that he had ex- amined me 6 months earlier and there were none. They had been surgically removed at age three.

At the time of these examinations I was shifting my internal health pictures. I realized on some level that I had wanted the Western medical professionals to acknowledge that miracles are possible and that we have more power then we know. But clearly that was not going to happen.

I love that I currently have representatives from the scientific and medical professions training with me as apprentices. I realize that it is important for me to step into my own authority and let go of attempting to 'prove' anything to non-believers.

If you begin with the understanding that visual challenges are correctable and that by clearing miasms (group thought virus) and poor DNA programs, many of the visual issues can be permanently corrected.

# MODULE SiX:
## DYNAMISM RESTORING EVERYTHING IN YOU THAT PRODUCES VITALITY AND POWER

# ENERGY AND OUR BODY

## Energy is All Around Us

There is a lot of talk about 'energy.' Whether as a fuel source or something of spirit, there is energy all around us. It is the most sought after of commodities and, at this point, is well paid for to control, enhance, and manufacture energy. Mobil oil and the 5-hour energy drink manufactures have a market on the new currency of life.

**What is energy?** Energy is the dynamic aspect of life that has no form or weight. It is light and movement. When you are filled with energy, you are capable of exerting your thoughts into physical reality.

My new exploration of cellular quantum mechanics points to a greater picture of energy than previously understood.

The program for the human blueprint and the miraculous system of energy support is encoded into the DNA. It starts its implementation as life begins. Chakras develop over a seven-year period, receiving their directions not only from the DNA program but also the aura, life force, spirit and golden rings!

How does proper distribution of energy support the body? A healthy life lived in balance with great energy will be a symphony of energy reserves accessed throughout the journey of existence.

## Golden Rings or Your Halo!

First, your halo, your golden rings, provides you with the energy to literally transform your health, and that of others, to vibrancy. It is the quantum cellular mechanics energy. When you have mastered the access to this energy and directed use of this energy, it is virtually without limits. You can use this source of golden light to restore energy centers in your physical and energetic body that are failing and generally juice up all the systems, even reverse the process of aging.

## Human Spirit

Human Spirit must be present in human animal for life to begin at birth. Surprisingly, large numbers of individuals do not get well established in their bodies and live connected as a spirit just through their head and part of their torso.

## Neurons

Brain, nerves and skin are fortified by healthy neurons. Neurons provide the current or electricity of the body. The neurons support movement as well as source energy to the five senses. You feel a feather across your skin from neuron responsiveness. Neurons provide the fuel needed for taste buds to receive and understand the information, for example.

## Chakras and Aura

The chakras and aura provide a great deal of support to specific areas in and around the body. The chakras, appearing like vortexes, flux in energetic fuel to the system, gland, or organ it is providing for.

The colors of the aura have a direct bearing on how you appear energetically to others. The dark colors drag you down physically, as well as spiritually, mentally and emotionally. Tuning up the seven layers of the auric field to bright colors can significantly assist you in feeling better, stronger, more vibrant, and more vital.

## Mitochondria

Mitochondria are the fuel source for the cell. It resembles a funny sort of caterpillar in appearance. Mitochondria are the cells' energy generator, the individualized fuel source for the cells.

## Muscles

Designed by DNA and enhanced by exercise and nutrition, the muscles in your body support power and perseverance. Think about someone who is called a weakling. They are small, under-developed and bring little to the table that is energetic. To have muscles and to use and keep muscles strong is much of what keeps us young and juiced up. Think of someone called muscle bound, or a muscle head. They are going to provide a ton of energy to a situation, perhaps moving mountains.

Join us on the Miraculous Living Radio show live Thursday morning 8 am PDT to learn more about your energy systems, receive a healing and a short meditation that will improve your overall body fuel and give you the power to enjoy your wonderful life right now!

# REFLECTiONS ON CLEARiNGS
# AND SUCCESSFUL MOMENTUM

Just two years ago it dawned on me, if I was not living my dream life, there was no one, no circumstances, nothing that was truly holding me back but myself and the answers to my challenges were ready to be known and understood.

Twenty-two months ago I was $200K in debt, having decided to not bring investors on as I poured money into Gable Kennedy (my company) and my vision. I had a knowing I was being Divinely guided and blessed. I did not feel the weight of the debt, only the certainty that it was indeed time to reveal what I had discovered about the human blueprint and the quantum field to all of humanity.

I knew that my simple beginnings had not prepared me to lead a global reach 7 figure company, but that my prayers to help humanity were being heard and with a powerful 'Grace' was to unfold how and what was to be done. Love and passion would get me to the next steps of my mission mastery.

Back then I was living in a little rental, a small very modest 2-bedroom condo on freeway 101. I paid $1300 a month rent and had lived there for fourteen years. When I moved in I thought I would heal from the accident that had left me in a wheel chair and buy a home. But I had more life challenges to pass through before I would make my way to realizing my dreams.

I had wanted children and had attempted fertility treatments and the 'works' on my own. Over time I experienced getting pregnant and losing the baby to miscarriages thirteen times. I spent a year preforming music with a famous Pakistani violinist, (that's a whole story in itself) but my path was not to stop helping others heal so I did return to my wellness practice.

I unfortunately had a bout of pre cervical cancer, awoke one day with strong guidance to have a hysterectomy or I would lose my life. The doctor who had been urging me for four years to take it out, finally had the opportunity to remove my very sick female parts. He was shocked to see the condition of my uterus from the severe radiation poisoning, it was unrecognizable. I had given him an account of what he would find just prior to surgery, and he poo pooed me saying I'll take photos, but it was exactly as I described it and he was a man completely in shock having decided not to take pictures as he had indicated I was being a hypochondriac prior to surgery on my notion of how severe the damage was.

About two years after this event I was engaged to a Japanese Pediatrician who got cold feet just before the big day, canceling our home purchase (we were in escrow) and calling off our plans to have the surrogate mother carry two babies for us. All the while I dreamed of a beautiful home in the country, a growing family with room for gatherings and family holidays.

One day in July 2014, a woman acquaintance informed me I was not going to have my dream, for many years. She was thought of as a kind of amateur fortune teller. She said to me I was unrealistic to imagine home, children, husband, family… global reach and becoming a world leader… she thought it could not be done.

I am so grateful she showed no vote of confidence in me as it was indeed a wake up call for me. I thought to myself: who had I been surrounding myself with and what had I not yet done to kick into gear and manifest my dream?

In November I was $80k in debt and qualified for a $59k mortgage. But I knew to power of 'Grace' would find a new way a miraculous way for me to realize my hearts desire. I was told by the realtor I worked with she couldn't show me million dollar plus homes because I hadn't qualified, I assured her I had the means to do the transaction when the time came. In November, feeling into my heart I saw a home, my home, in a village I had never been to. I saw I would move to Carmel Valley and realize the dream. This was 100% true. Have you ever had this happen, an unstoppable certainty of an unlikely future that must be fulfilled?

The powers of heaven and earth moved as the first home I viewed on my tour the first day out, blew my mind! This was not just a house, this was a dream realized. As I walked up the stairs, with the breath taking views and open floor plan and all the features I imagined and more—OMG OMG OMG!!! My home had found me where I wasn't looking and I had felt into my heart to get my answer.

The summit interviews were so helpful providing a new larger platform to teach and mentor. Also in realizing the dream, and bringing my income and 'bundle' of cash to the amount needed to get in. I put down 30% with all debts paid off and easily secured a seven figure mortgage. I went back and forth with reluctant sellers who had owned the house since it was built and they finally after four weeks of negotiating they finally said yes. I moved in three months later and have now been here thirteen months.

What is amazing is all the dreams I had for this home are reality. Big thanksgiving and Christmas gatherings, Weeklong Retreats and workshops are held here with the most loving wonderful people on the planet, I am well into the process of adopting and am happily dating (ladies this is a wonderful area for single men... more men than women here!)

I had wanted to bring the Gable Kennedy to a place where I was doing more with teaching mentoring and training then just the one to one work I am so well known for, and brought on a productions staff to accomplish a dream of a global reach with 3 to 5 classes taught weekly now, some as large as 450 students, and growing, with the free community trainings reaching up to 1800 registered participants.

We have a team of 20 people working with my corporation Gable Kennedy. First Priority 5 million minds uplifted in this new awareness, next a global restoration of the earth. Business centered goals include moving the company status to a top female owned US corporation, and receive a Nobel prize for contributions to a global community.

I feel like this birthday April 24th, I am turning one year old, as my life began anew just a year back when I was able to step into the life I had always imagined for myself. I am so thrilled with the Your Year of Miracles, Immersion trainings and now the Apprentice on line certification, I know with absolute certainty the work I was charged to bring to the global community is being fully realized.

I am driven by love and an intense desire to help lift humanity to a higher field vibrationally. I want to help fade away the constrictions of the past for all people and to step into a golden age of love, wisdom, and spiritual power.

# SERENE GRACE iN AN ACTivE WORLD

As I pondered the meaning and presence of life, my thoughts went to the idea of stillness or silence. What is it truly to have the 'peace that passes all understanding?' is it just a quiet mind or is there more to this peace of God?

In the stillness, In the quiet,
In the open heart, there I am.
I am essence, I am breathe,
I am light of God, I am I am.

Let's start by imagining the presence and meaning of four key words related to internal quiet.

Silence ~ quiet lacking inner and out chatter
Stillness ~ without movement or action
Serenity ~ awareness of perfection and ease in the state of im-
perfection
Peace ~ a state of grace and a calmness of heart

These are not dictionary definitions, but rather notions of truth resonating in the ethers, coming through to my own quiet mind.

Starting with Silence we think of quietude. In this quiet there is no inner or out chatter. Silence is the gift we give ourselves, often while in the presence of divinity. Perhaps you would experience it following active prayer, meditation or chanting. Simon and Garfunkel immortalized this idea, "echo's the sound of silence,' though I am guessing this deeper peace may not have been part of the motivations behind the song lyrics. Knowing the highest vibration of silence is knowing joyous vibrations of Divinity.

When we are in Stillness we are without movement or action. It reflects the expressions of the body, the opposite of movement, and requires a stilling of the muscles, a relaxing of active body. Motion ends and stillness begins. For some, the only time they are really still is in sleep. There is a great blessing in experiencing stillness, spirit in body. The aligning and attuning spirit to an unmoving body can strengthen ones life force and restore purpose in a time of loss.

Serenity requires a person who has at some point lacked 'peace of mind.' With serenity one has both awareness of emotions in an idyllic or perfected state and ease in living in the state of emotional imperfection.

Peace as a state of being reflects an individual filled with grace and a wearing a calmness of heart. Can peace be more than the opposite of war, hatred and fighting? Can it align the hearts of all to loving kindness generosity and true charity? All I think yes. Which brings us back to a scripture quote: the peace that passeth all understanding. This is a peace of Divine connection. Peace that is not responsive to the lack of, but rather the blessing brought from a disciplined balance spiritual life. From a life of love and serviced balanced by times of reflection and calm quiet mind. I wish this deep peace for you.

# MODULE SEvEN:
## CLEARING PAIN

# WHAT YOU DO WiTH CHALLENGE DETERMiNES YOUR OUTCOME

From time to time, everyone faces adversity and trial. What you do with that adversity will affect the quality and happiness of your life. Will you choose a path of blaming, "meaning making" or personal responsibility? Depression or elation can come out of the same adversity. It's time to ask yourself, "Which response would I rather choose?"

Many of my clients seeking to feel and be 100% healthy share with me how a difficult relationship they had with a parent or relative has affected how they view the world and their ability to feel the freedom needed to live life large and powerful. Childhood abuse, physical or sexual, is a common theme in these conversations. It is one we are not taught how to deal with. Given no real guidance, these circumstances often produce the inability to forgive and move out of darkness into light.

Here are three possible responses and interpretations to this challenge. You will notice that how the loss of personal power—freedom to express their authentic self and the freedom for emotional bliss—expansive living can come from the exact same situation.

## Anger, Resentment and Bitterness

Have you met someone who carries a banner of pain and suffering in their very essence? This person will have a response/belief system that is based on blame and lack. The individual feels that the odds are stacked against them and they use the incident or problem as an excuse to avoid being more than they are. They want others to make exceptions for them and they live in an unreal world, where their lack of success is someone else's fault. They are blind to the natural order of business and miss both an important mental attitude as well as appropriate timely action to accomplish their task. They are depressed and disappointed when life doesn't give them what they 'deserve.' They are fond of thinking of themselves as a good person, innocent and, on some level, in their imaginations they have done everything they could to succeed, yet success is obscure and unrealized.

You are not wrong if you are in this position. But, as you can see, you are in a weakened condition and are prone to struggle. Physical, emotional, mental and spiritual struggle are encompassed in this 'thought form.' You cannot truly succeed because you have a thought form dominating your consciousness that is against the natural order of abundance and joy.

## Fuel from the Struggle

The second response to the problem is to believe that you are powerless, but you will turn lemons into lemonade. You think the problem is a difficulty or curse that you had nothing to do with creating, yet you are churning the adversity into something you can show others you have overcome. You get fuel from the struggle. You publicly 'show and tell' people that this problem is one that you have nothing to do with. You are versed partially in the law of attraction so you are turning the failure into fertilizer for your better future.

In many ways, this second choice is what we, as a culture, understand best. We are listening to hear this kind of a story from those who touch, move and inspire us. The mess to success story helps us to relate to another who is 'just like me' somehow. This is an excellent place to speak from for the general populace to understand the concept of turning adversity into something good or even great. If you tell your story understanding and implementing the third approach to embracing adversity, you will have the most power.

## Personal Responsibility

The third response, perhaps less popular but by far the most powerful response, is to take responsibility for what has happened. With no blame, anger, or resentment present, you create the thought form of greatness and a vibratory response of truth.

This step requires the space of emotional generosity and a willingness to understand a much bigger picture. You cannot respond this way if you have not fueled your emotional tanks. You must love yourself so much that you know everything coming to you was designed perfectly to give you what you needed for full enlightenment and full ascension in this body.

Begin to step into this phase of truth by asking:

- What is it I wanted to have happen from this experience?
- What did I seek to learn from it?
- How did I want to grow?
- What is the highest interpretation of this challenge?
- Did I need something huge to wake me up to my divinity, something that would be so far from who I know myself to be that I could say, I am not that?!

100% Healthy is possible when you really go for it. Try new things. Take more responsibility than you possibly could. Fuel your emotional tanks. Life is a daring adventure or nothing at all. Live to your greatest potential. Love to your fullest capacity and pursue 100% of your healthy life every single day!

# YOUR AHA MOMENT

Open your heart and allow love in....

Realizing you are not as healthy as you might have thought, you have a wake up moment and declare "this is my time." For example, time to put me first and foremost and, if it's not too late, give it a good effort to (a) get my weight in check, (b) get my nerves unscrambled and/or (c) my mind out of fuzz brain mode.

Sometimes this happens at the beginning of the year, around the time of New Year's resolutions, but it is not the only time you might become aware of declining or struggling health issues.

When you get to this point, you have likely waited too long and you will have a longer journey back to health.

Quiz to identify the key factors for health breakdown:

1. Do you have a habit of pushing through even when your body needs rest?
2. Do you skip breakfast or other meals to squeeze 'it' all in?
3. Do you exercise too much or too little trying to make up for a life out of balance?

4. Do you laugh often, or can't remember when you had your last belly laugh?
5. Do you regularly get 8 hours of restful sleep?
6. Do you rely on coffee and energy drinks to get you through the afternoon?
7. Are you stressed beyond belief?
8. When was your last real vacation? Is your next vacation scheduled?
9. Are you living with gratitude on the tip of your tongue or disappointment, frustration, or disillusionment?

Great health comes from a great mindset and excellent habits. Many writers have studied the habits of wealthy and successful people. Perhaps we should also be paying attention to the habits of vibrantly healthy, happy individuals.

The seeds to a 100% healthy life come from appreciation and gratitude at the core of our being laced with an awesome lifestyle including daily meditation, walks in nature, good eating habits, clean fresh drinking water and fun! If you love your vocation, you are indeed one of the fortunate ones. If you are struggling in work, decide to let go of the struggle and find your way to a vocation you love.

Let your "aha moments" be the fuel for new beginnings and positive changes that will provide the ground for a long and healthy, vibrant life.

# TEN THiNGS DOCTORS DON'T KNOW ABOUT CHRONiC PAiN AND WHAT YOU CAN DO TO FEEL BETTER RiGHT NOW

You were born a happy, healthy little person, ready to bring on your biggest, best ever life. You progressed through your life and at some time the glow and happy enthusiasm faded and your health began to deteriorate. Over the past nineteen years, we at Miraculous Healing have assisted our clients in feeling better in their body regardless of the cause of the pain. We have helped reduce and eliminate pain from illness, injury, nerve damage, and broken bones. In the following paragraphs, we explore where pain comes from when it seems mysterious and we show how to rapidly shift your circumstances to feeling vibrant and healthy again. We've identified nine causes of persistent pain (or other ailing conditions) and their possible solutions. At the end of this article is an action plan that you can take now to help move you away from the problem.

1. No Nucleus (brain) in the cells affected by pain.
   How can there be no nucleus, you ask? Without a nucleus, the cell has no brain, no direction. Medical treatment is

responsible for 60% of the missing nuclei; toxicity and pollution ingested through air, water and food for 23%; medical illnesses, including a nasty bug called a mycoplasma for 15%; and a small percentage is actually congenital.

**Solution to No Nucleus (brain) in the cells.**

To replace the nucleus is definitely doable, but not through traditional Western medicine. In our Miraculous Living Apprentice program, we learn to harness our creator god force. This is the way we replace the nucleus.

Focus gold energy actively in the place where the nucleus used to be; over a few minutes the nucleus will again reappear and as gold energy continues to be focused into the nucleus, it will ultimately appear again at $100\%$.

2. Spiritual body failure.

During injuries and illness, the 264 chakras and mini chakras called nadis can fail, stop, be chopped off, and go altogether missing. Your body is meant to have energy moving in and out of the glands, organs and systems through these channels. That energy is an important part of the nourishment of the physical body.

**Solution to Spiritual Body Failure.**

The seven main body chakras are the priority.

Chakra one is found at the perineum. It is your base or survival chakra. The best colors here are deep green and red.

Chakra two is out the front of the body just above the pubic bone and out the back two inches up from the base of the spine/coccyx. This is the chakra of physical creativity and sensuality. The best colors in this chakra are peach, pink, orange and green.

Chakra three is about two inches up from the belly button and directly out the back. This chakra is related to will and power/energy. The best colors are green and red.

Chakra four is the heart chakra, two inches up from the base of the sternum and out the back. For women you can find it around your bra line. The best colors are red, pink, peach and all green.

Chakra five is at the base of the neck, in front and in back of the neck. It is the chakra of communication. The best colors are pink, green and yellow.

Chakra six is the brow or center of head chakra, often referred to as the third eye. It is out the front of the head between the eyebrows and out the back of the head three inches above where the spine meets the skull. The best color is a deep blue, followed closely by emerald green.

Chakra seven is your crown chakra and is your direct communication with the divine. The color is gold or yellow and should only be these colors.

We address many more of the spiritual body elements in the Miraculous Living Apprentice program. Having these seven chakras tuned and running well can really help feed the body energy and reduce pain.

3. Emotional Body Atrophy.

Painful emotions embed in the cells of your body and turn the light off in the cells. These painful emotions in the cells are a death energy that prevent the cells from returning to vibrancy and health.

Solution to Emotional Body Atrophy.

Painful emotions embed in the cells of your body and turn the light off in the cells. These painful emotions in the cells are a death energy that prevents the cell's return to vibrancy and health. We have a program for clearing emotional pain and love entanglements. The best thing to do now is to sit and breathe into the location where the pain is and allow it to move. This takes patience. The common places for this atrophy are liver, kidney, spleen, heart and intestines.

Private session with Julie Renee or one of her certified miraculous healers will be instrumental in clearing these hidden culprits.

4. Brain Patterns (Conscious)
Holding pain is a familiar feeling. Pain can become a companion and a quiet friend. When asking a pain client, "Would you like the pain taken from your body now, at no cost?" I was told, "No thanks, my life is designed around my pain. Everything I do and how I do it is paced around this condition and things would change too much for me."

5. Brain Patterns (Unconscious)
These are programs of influential people and related to how you are loved and given emotional encouragement and support.

6. Emotional Manipulation (Unconscious).
Get a payoff/something from this condition. May hold others hostage, gives a level of control and dominance. Get attention from others. Shame is often experienced. In this situation, your body is trained not to improve.

DNA patterns create a predisposition to having pain patterns like family members.

7. Emotional Family Bubble.
The "what you are suppose to feel at a certain age" syndrome, as in old, achy, tired, in pain and headaches. This is

sourced from the constant conversation that is subtle. When you hear it, your cells start matching the aches to make the person speaking correct, knowing it has to be fulfilled.

8. Nerve Pain.

Nerve pain is miserable and backing out of nerve pain means getting your body into the parasympathetic mode as much as possible and speaking to the nerves with love appreciation and gratitude. Great headway can be made by receiving ML brain healings in order to create entirely new directions for the nerves and the body to respond to. The guided meditation found in the "From Fatigued to Fabulous" free gift (julierenee.com) can help move you away from the sympathetic to the parasympathetic mode of the nervous system.

9. Mental Body Shadow Pain.

A phantom floating pain that lives in the physical body and shifts through the mental body, which is similar to the spiritual imprint on the cellular body.

10. Solutions to Brain Patterns (Conscious) and Action Plan

This is holding pain as a familiar 'feeling.' If you notice that this is your challenge, the first thing you need to do is make a list of all the things you get... or benefit from..., by having ongoing pain. I get free... I get attention from... I have friendships bonded from pain... Really be honest and write as many "wins" as possible from this condition. Next, write all the things you might have to deal with, or face, or new ways of being, you would need to create, if life shifted. Finally write down all the things you could do, be, have and accomplish, if pain were not an issue in your life.

List One—How I benefit from this condition You will need to let go of each, one by one and completely in order to move to

List Two—New challenges I have to face if I no longer have this condition.

List Two turns into a strategy list; a list of "how do I find a solution or get help from others to find a solution for these circumstances that will need to be embraced and overcome?"

List Three—all the things you could do, be, or accomplish if this condition were not a part of your life.

These can really be felt, once List One and Two have been fully addressed. Then List Three is full to catapult you in the most freeing way to your life; the life of grace and ease, the life you have only dreamed of and can now truly be a real possible future.

List One, I benefit from having pain...

1.

2.

3.

List more on a fresh sheet; continue until you have entirely emptied out.

# THREE SiMPLE STEPS TO MANiFESTiNG A FULLY iNTEGRATED APPROACH TO BEiNG HEALTHY

## Life in Balance

Do you find it hard to keep life in balance and health optimal with your active demanding life?

Being healthy isn't about getting there; it's about 'getting there,' 'staying there' and increasing the great health every day. This may be completely counter intuitive to your current mindset.

If the goal is to 'get healthy' what happens after that? It's kind of like the dieter who starves himself or herself, accomplishes their ideal weight, and just like Oprah on her first dip down and yoyo back, once the goal is met, the drive disappears and the weight or poor health returns.

The new health model is sustainable health, 100% Healthy, wealthy and in love with being you for a lifetime.

You may be like many of my One day clients who are healthy but know they could feel much better and are ready to take a big shift up. Just having this attitude is going to get the shift started. I love working with people and getting them to their 100% healthy whether in a One day program or a year-long 100% healthy program; if you need to raise the bar and have health set at a higher level, this is a great approach.

So once you've moved to the level of health that makes your life rock, sustainability is the next important step.

## Master Your Mindset

Mindset is the most important piece in this quest. Be strong, be healthy and be alive. Engage in your life with passion and direction. Keep your mind and heart on what is great about your life and focus your attentions on GOD. GOD is the sum total of everything beautiful and wonderful in your life, each and every day!

## Healthy Lifestyle

Eat, sleep and exercise for your optimum health benefit. Healthy food and super foods with healthy water and enough water is an important part of loving the body and keeping it well. Sleep eight hours a night; let your body really regenerate. Use your body in fun and energizing ways with a healthy lifestyle of cardio, weights and stretching. Take vacations. Love your life and what you do when you are earning money.

## The Fountain of Youth is Meditation

To really be great, to clear all the energy channels and stressors from the body, I recommend you meditate at least 30 minutes a day. Using our guided meditations you will easily clear stress and challenge from the body rapidly. I also suggest you do meditation in nature as often as possible. This is in addition to your guided session. Walking in nature heals you, restores your negative and positive ions to balance and centers you for healthy emotions. If you have too much energy in your mental body, this act of meditation in nature will bring the metal body back down to balance.

100% healthy doesn't mean that something might come up that needs adjusting. Just like a car you wouldn't drive it 100,000 miles without a brake pad change. If your DNA triggers a health issue, just respond right away in an authentic natural course. Drugs will not cure a health problem. You have to go inside to correct the issue.

Achieving a life of 100% health and vitality means living in balance.

Having the spiritual emotional mental and physical aspects of life well nurtured. I invite you to think about the blessings of being in a supportive community as you return to health and set your new lifestyle habits in place.

Julie Renee's Year of Miracles year-long health activation program prepares you for a lifetime of vibrant health!

# NERvE REGENERATiON:
# THE SOLUTiON FOR NEUROPATHY,
# ANXiETY, AND PARKiNSON'S DiSEASE

In this age of quantum health activations things previously thought impossible are now becoming a reality. We are experiencing tremendous breakthroughs and what would be considered miraculous results in our nerve regeneration process.

The conversation around nerve regeneration starts with pure science. We look to the Stanford genetic scientists exploring the regeneration of skin stem cells. In the Crabtree laboratory at Stanford the scientists are diligently working on a process of taking skin stem cells and cultivating them into human nerve cells in sterile laboratory conditions. We know that skin, brain, and nerve cells are formed early on from the same embryonic materials, so this make perfect sense.

While visiting with my friend and top Genetic Scientist Jerry Crabtree who is the head of Crabtree laboratory he explained why this break through is so exciting. Being able to turn skin stem cells into nerve stem cells means 15 or 20 years down the road science may be able to replace a full nervous system! Hundreds of miles of nerves would be available for folks who have illnesses that currently have no cure like Parkinson's disease.

I am excited for science and the exploration of what is possible and it seems to go hand in hand with what we are accomplishing using the quantum field and the human blueprint. I have developed protocols yielding incredible results for students and clients that are yielding truly amazing results and some pretty miraculous transformations.

The protocols for nerve regeneration include clearing programs in the field of amplification, perception and emotions that are informing the nerves to malfunction or function at less than optimal performance. In this first step, we remove the programs of disease and illness. Unlike science we also remove the soul contracts, curses, past life influences and emotions that directly influence the nerves.

In addition to these clearings we perform DNA Obliteration, which is the removal of poor performance DNA encoding informing the body to experience nerve issues. This DNA process has cleared cancer DNA, Alzheimer's and other debilitating genetically influenced illnesses freeing up clients to live with greater ease knowing they no longer have these influences that can potentially spring up as full blown illness.

Step two includes the removal of unwanted energies, entities, and dominant dark patterns in the nerves. Again we are addressing things that science may not have a container for. And yet the individuals are very aware that not all of what is happening to them is them.

Step three in the process of completely healing the nerves and restoring them to their healthy state is cellular neo genesis. This is the actual regeneration of the nerve stem cells. Cellular Neo Genesis includes the restoration of the master stem cell to 100%. This technique requires the use of the quantum field and   human blue print. Once the nerve master stem cell is restored to 100% it is mirrored to the surrounding cells. This step improves the immediate function of the system. What is truly exciting to me is the actual nerve regeneration. With the 100% healthy Master cell a program is activated in the mitochondria starting a cascade of new cell growth! This final step continues to produce new nerve cells for many days often 70–140 days! Growing a restoring the current malfunctioning nerves to health once more.

Early in the development of cell regeneration, I thought that the regeneration of nerves was more difficult and took longer than the regeneration of other kinds of cells. What I've discovered is that nerve cells are highly intelligent and responsive cells that are intensely affected by all programming and energetic influences. If time is taken up front to remove all the programming and un-wanted energetic influences, then the nerves return to their healthy state once more. Making nerve regeneration a viable and powerful procedure with amazing results.

It is important to note that nerves are so directly connect to what is happening in the brain that I have found the best nerve restoration results follow a full brain regeneration.

Neuropathy, nervousness and anxiety as well as Parkinson's and all nerve related illnesses are greatly improved by this process. I've had the joy of helping two lovely women get the feeling back in legs and feet as well as restoring a traumatic brain injury pa- tient his feeling in legs and feet. A Pentagon employee who suffered from panic and anxiety was completely cured of her struggles with this technique. And a Parkinson's sufferer experience wonderful re-lief and a slowing of symptoms. This was years ago what's so excit-ing is I have discovered more of the pieces to solving the mystery of nerve illnesses and I now have many new techniques that address the issues in that had remained unknowable until now.

Nerve regeneration is possible!

# MODULE EiGHT:
## LOVE

# SHE WHO WOULD BE KiNG

I work with so many high powered, wonderful women who are making their business dreams come true and feeling a bit lost and lonely in the journey. It's a new day; it's a new dawn and a step for women in executive and leadership roles in the direction of the 'undiscovered territory.' This game changer (large numbers of women in leadership roles) marks the beginning of a new chapter in human history.

Female leadership and the rise of successful women in the global economy is currently sky rocketing

And with this rising new era of empowered women, unique new challenges spring up. Some of these challenges include; loss of family structure, a loss of relatedness, and an entire population of females running businesses and staying alone.

Yesterday, on my client Kimberly's third VIP 100% One Day she spilled the beans. She has been running a high-end, powerful corporate speaking and consulting business. Kimberly's blessing is in her pure genius as she developed a rare and poignant specialty that commands upwards of $30,000 per speech. She   oversees her magnificent arsenal including; speaking and coaching tools in place, a system of delivery, and most importantly a willing audience that has kept her hopping. The downside to this, however, is she finds herself sad, lonely and out of balance. She has taken the position of King and, in her world; it is not safe for a woman in power, competing against male kings, to have a fun time. Her work ethics and values cause the work driven leader to be isolated, alone and imprisoned in a life without a loving partnership.

In the leadership role as director, producer and superstar of her life her ground rules include; overworking, being the best and striving. On the contrary, activities that might be fun are in her perception a waste of time. She literally has no personal permission for fun. Kimberly is on the island of pain (and misfit queens) in the role she has chosen to live as  King.

## Woman as King

When a woman lives in her male brain during the day, she is living into; focus, concentration and results. She may develop in her nature attributes like; competition, directness, a hard edge and even aggression. While these male qualities emerge and take root, her softer side must be set to the wayside for her survival in the male driven world of  business.

## Julie Renee Gives Relationship Advice to Women.

It is possible to run a Queendom from the throne of King, but it will take a commitment to preserving balance and letting go of competition outside of work. We relate competition, which is innately a male trait, with performance excellence. It can help a woman to lead efficiently, but this male style of relating will prevent the much longed for bond for her in a romantic partnership.

## Qualities Lost When the Queen Lives as a King Night and Day

A king (one who rules a domain—be it office, company or farmstead) in a male body has less need for social life. In comparison a female attempting to be king is dominated by her estrogen based social brain will needs healthy interaction to maintain a healthy, happy demeanor. Getting a female king to take a vacation, or spend time in frivolous pursuits goes against the nature of striving. Male kings may naturally sink into a lifestyle striving as he builds and extends the reaches of his kingdom.

Now any man, king or not, is warmed by the quality of social interaction found in the company of a queen. Men become enthusiastic about a potential partner's beauty, graciousness and especially the sense of comfort he feels in her presence.

If, however, a woman is edgy, sharp or competitive around a potential 'mate,' she is not sending the signals for a man to bond with her. Realize this: a man is not looking to mate with another king.

What then is he seeking? Someone to support him for example, I often hear men say about the woman they love; 'she's got my back'. Another quality they seek is to enhance or make more wondrous his domain. Along these same lines a fella is looking to provide for his gal, and also protect her. For him, this is his measure of how close they are and how well he is doing in his job as partner. If you mistakenly thought the fella you were dating wanted you to be self- sufficient, (a mistake I have made more than once I'm sad to say) I hate to tell you, but you were wrong. Self—sufficiency to a man means you have no need for him.

Please don't confuse that concept of fierce independence with your nature of competence or capability. They are not the same. If you want to be independent, then think about the meaning of the word. If that holds true for you after you have given it some consideration you will be delighted to discover there are plenty of willing participants for the occasional tryst. Just stop lying to yourself that you want a long-term partnership. You will be happier to love what you have than to create an impossible scenario.

## How to Return to Your Queen's Throne?

Step back into balance and begin by affirming your love and trust, and give yourself permission to express your unique self every day. Once that's done, it's time to get into action.

Best tips for recovering your juicy, loving self

1. Play time. If your emotional tanks are not fueled you will be edgy, irritable or dismissive. The challenge you may temporarily be experiencing of no sweetheart is about you. Good or bad, it's always about you. You can think of playtime as part of your job requirements and start implementing play dates. Create some dates with friends, groups, and fun family connections. Be sure to also create time for you to enjoy the company of yourself. If you don't know how to have fun, or you think having fun is hard, or feels like work you may have a program in your DNA stopping you from fun. This harmful program can be removed through the process of DNA Obliteration. You can request this as part of your VIP 100% You! One Day. (Tell me more 100%)

2. Check your King's crown at the door. If you are in a position where it is best to be King at work, you must, must, must take off the King's crown as you end your workday and get back to you as queen. This might be done in a simple action of changing into relaxed, or feminine clothing or using a Beauty Meditation to get you back to feeling your gorgeous girlie self. The important thing is to put your sword down… the sword meaning the nature of competition. You

don't need it to have a loving successful relationship, and as a matter of fact, if you drag that blade into your love life, prepare for severing it at some point sooner or later.

3. When you are around men, look for the qualities of protection, providing and serving that you can revel in and enjoy. Be the appreciator. Let go of the perception that all men are dangerous, jerks or harmful in some way and look to each man as on a path to being your or someone else's hero. Make a practice of thanking each kind and helpful act you are cultivating from the gentlemen around you. Get that you too are a mystery to them

In 1983 I participated in the EST programs. (This was the original training of Warner Erhard and eventually was called the Landmark Forum.)Through the years as the programs developed, the concept of being responsible for how people show up in your space became an important part of the teachings.

## Experiment

Sit next to a friend who is in agreement with you to do this. Have the friend talk to you about something they are excited, perhaps passionate, about. While the friend is speaking, think as strongly as possible, "You are stupid, your ideas are stupid. What a nut, I don't believe you."

Now after two minutes stop, and ask your passionate friend what they felt as they spoke to you. Change places and repeat the exercise.

It is unpleasant, even repulsive to share your 'pearls with swine.' It would be ridiculous to share your treasures with someone who is not on the same page with you, or at least honoring your journey.

Who shows up when you are with a fella?

The last concept builds on the previous one. Are your emotional tanks full and are you feeling emotionally generous? If you have been doing battle as King, then show up in that space of perception; who are you being and what is it bringing out in the fella you are sharing time with?

I know that you may want to hold onto your power, and you can if you want to create separation; to be in partnership means being receptive to your beloved. Have you ever noticed a man in love? How it almost appears he has become the servant of his beloved. They are happy, joyous and juicy together. It seems like they are privy to a sexy secret as they wink at each other and smile knowingly.

You can't be a king and a queen at the same time. That's all there is to it.

# MODULE NiNE:
# CLEARING AND REGENERATING

# WHAT YOU DON'T KNOW COULD HURT YOU: THREE RAPiD AGiNG ACTiviTiES TO AvOiD

## Live a Healthy Lifestyle!

Getting it right and living a 100% healthy active lifestyle is simple and easy when you know what to put your attention on and how to improve your LIQ (Longevity IQ). I am often surprised to discover the unconsciousness present in creating life. It is as if people think it would take a great deal of effort to live a superior life. Living a 100% healthy lifestyle takes little effort and provides fuel for a life of greatness and vitality.

1. Pre Sleep Disposition

   Have you gone to bed stressed or angry? If so, you are going to bed with an aging pattern set to keep you on the fast track to lines, wrinkles and exhaustion. I know you are likely exhausted and you just want to stop—drop and dose but this is not the answer. Attempt to keep a sunny disposition during your day. If someone rains on your parade later in the day, you can still turn it around by declaring no one gets to change your mood. Take charge. The use of the Definitive Guide to

Karma Clearing meditation is great to shift the energy and regain control. Going to be in a relaxed state, with your nerves in parasympathetic mood means your cells are set to regenerate, refresh and restore. Going to bed angry upset or in distress means your nerves are set on high alert, energy is going to survival and the nerves in this position will not allow energy to flow in the refresh mode.

2. You Can Choose How to Fuel Your Day
   Is this jangling you awake?

Imagine waking up 5:49 am to a blaring alarm. You hit the snooze six times and groggily arise, stubble to the bathroom, splash cold on your face, turn on some tunes, while the news streams between songs commercials blare and you're out the door for the local coffee shop for your first caffeine injection of the day.

Or:

You arise naturally; start the day with a glass of pure glacier water and settle in for a 20-minute meditation. You arise from meditation and head out the door for a delightful power walk around a mountain lake. As you walk you stream through all the things you are grateful for, all the people you love and who love you; you affirm your beautiful life, breathe deeply, imagine a wonderful day full of successful connections and lots of laughter.

As in number one, if you live the first version you age yourself, by straining the adrenals, nerves and general constitution. Pushing through the day is a very different experience than breathing into the day, in celebration. You choose.

3. Busy or Active

The word busy is a stress word. When you are informing others you are busy you are riding the waves of stress. Busy means not enough time to integrate and relax. It is a version of slavery, you may be the slave driver and the slave, but I promise you if you are saying you are busy you are not happy.

Try experimenting with the word Active and see how that changes your perception of reality. Active denotes, chose, it indicates a level of good health and a kind of happy excitement. The difference in these two words means the difference in being the joyous creator of your life and lifestyle or the out of control slave who is unawake and unaware of the truly wonderful life just out of reach.

Choose the high road to be 100% healthy.

You decide. It is like this in all areas of life, you can take the high road or the low road. The low road ages you, depletes you, and robs you of your happiness vitality and joy. Living the low version takes away the potential for greatness and adds the complication of struggle and depletion. On the other hand living 100% healthy is the road to life of magnificence, creation energy and joy. You will be connected and in love with your life as you move from slave to creator. It is not either or, they are two separate realms. Who have you been recently? Who are you committing to be now?

## Recommended

**The Definitive Guide to Karma Clearing:** Take the emotional charge out of difficult relationships and free yourself and the other person to enjoy each other.

**Love Regeneration and Walking Meditation:** Exercise while you meditate to save time and get into a space of loving and gratitude.

# SEvEN FUNDAMENTALS FOR LiviNG AN EXTRAORDiNARY LiFE!

Live an extraordinary life!

I am often asked how I am able to live such a rich and full life despite the intense illness and the ups and downs mentally and emotionally from having multiple cancers and 17 surgeries. Along the way to 100% health, I've discovered the secret path to living an extraordinary life. Your existence is not defined by the complicated set of circumstances life brings you. Rather, living an extraordinary life is a conscious choice to be and become your greatness.

I have discovered seven fundamental elements of life that when engaged to the fullest expression will result in 100% human fulfillment. This is your guide to life well lived.

1. Vitality—having a great cellular constitution
   Your vitality and energetic presence give you the winning edge. When you are healthy, people around you feel safe and confident. More than that, you feel unstoppable. You are able to make plans and follow through with great velocity

and intention. Enjoying a healthy body is the most important element, as it creates the ground from which you can soar. Without good health you live a life pieced together, built on a shaky foundation.

2. Alignment and purpose

Alignment with your spiritual journey and connection with source is the second element of living an extraordinary life. To be in alignment will require you to take time away from the hustle and bustle of life and the pressures of group mind and family agreements The greatest quest you can engage in is to discover who you are and what you are up to in this life. To live authentically, you must know who you are and why you are here. Making your best guess or operating on autopilot is not good enough. Make time for you to know you.

3. Discipline to strength

A person who knows disciple is able to fulfill their mission and gains the respect of all those who they come in contact with. Discipline is the path to fulfillment of everything made manifest. To be healthy, wealthy and wise you must engage in a strategic discipline. Personal power comes from the ability to follow through. You can only experience discipline when you have cleared the entire muddle and 'squirrels'/distractions from your path. You must first fuel yourself, meaning you must fill yourself up to emotional fulfillment. When you are filled up you have a greater capacity to be emotional generous with yourself and all others.

4. Enthusiasm for truth

When you blend enthusiasm with truth you open to your greatest expression of self. As you enthusiastically call truth to you, you continue your journey towards awakening to your divine nature and powerful access to miraculous energies. Enthusiasm lights the way to higher wisdom. The one caveat to this conversation is to not get caught up with your version of truth. When truth has an opinion it is actually a belief rather than an absolute. Truth has no other version. It just is.

5. Ascension the progress of your awakening

The journey of ascension does not require you to consciously drive towards spiritual awakening. In this case your balanced loving life will move you towards your ascension. I now see the opportunity for full enlightenment, which includes mastery in the spiritual realm as well as the emotional, mental and physical realms, is a deeper richer type of enlightenment then just a spiritual awakening. The old awakening model was to throw all your intention into a spiritual journey and remove yourself from the world so as to gain enlightenment. This is still a valid journey, but a higher enlightenment of the human experience is the mastery of all aspects of your life leaving nothing behind.

6. Mindset—Love-magic—Love-wisdom

Joy and bliss includes having fun.

To have your mind in the right place makes all the difference in living an extraordinary life. Having the brain working well with all the neurotransmitters and chemistry supporting your joyous bliss filled life is a vital part of your successful experience. When you are in love with your life and with all those who you interact with you have mastered your mindset and your life. Remember a healthy brain gives you the ground for healthy emotions.

The awareness of the oneness of all things is the mystery and the doorway to glory.

7. Connection—love appreciation

This leads us into the final element and the bookend that holds this magnificent formula together. Appreciation for everything and everyone is the greatest lesson and expression of human kind. Love is always the answer. If your days are filled with gratitude and appreciation for the wonderful life you are now living, even if some days are not so wonderful, staying with the grace of appreciation will install the deepest connection to the Divine and to the greatness majesty and wonder of humankind.

Living into your 100% life means living an exemplary life. You will become the guiding light to your friends and followers as you show the well-lit path towards the ever-unfolding magnificent existence. You choose. Know that you have always had the opportunity to choose. Now I invite you to consciously make a choice for greatness. Join me in living an extraordinary life, and be filled with the peace and bliss that surpasses thought or mental understanding. Be.

# SPRiNG THEORY: THE PROGRESSiON OF TiME AS EXPERiENCED BY THE HUMAN PSYCHE iN A NON-LiNEAR EvOLUTiON

## Part One

Several years ago I found myself exploring my recorded history and experience of time as I progressed through a 5 mile run around my favorite pristine mountain lake. I was at peace. The crystal clear stillness of the lake seemed to expand my access to Divine mind and higher concepts of the natural and super natural world. As my steps moved forward on the rugged trail my fifth brain was actively pondering concepts of time. I noticed time which had become our standard human measure was accurately responsive to 'time mechanisms' like clocks and timers, yet did not seem to progress at the same rate. There were days that flew by at an accelerated rate and seemed to be experienced in a quarter of the regular day: while other days crawled by at a snail's pace and seemed doubly long.

## in the Stillness

In the Stillness
In the quiet
In the open heart
There I am
I am essence
I am breath
I am light of God
I am I am
—2003

As I reflected I could attribute some of the anomalies in the experience of time speeding up could be attributed to an organized schedule with a focused list of accomplishments needing fulfillment, while other times the state of emotions/the psyche could seem to slow time as depression or sadness ruled, or sped up as excitement and love seems to accelerate time.

The idea of time management made sense: if one was out to accomplish a great amount in a specific cycle of a day or week or for that matter any cycle supported by a plan of completion, this structured time would seem to command the powers of time. And the opposite unstructured time would play out as influenced by the thought forms and momentum of previous cycles or influencing factors.

So understanding the lassoing of time by a structured plan explained part of my experience of time bending but there were other occurrences I had observed that would not fall under this explanation.

Access to the concept time bending from the previous discussion in the most linear of exploration is affected by the human mind and the belief or need to accomplish tasks or perhaps dally in difficult emotion.

All time variances are experienced in the field of amplification. In the simplest understanding of this field it is the field law of attraction enthusiasts use to draw all good to them. It supports an accelerated drive towards manifesting in all realms of human needs, wants and desires. It is not limited to the physical accelerations and can be a great force for change. The Realm of Amplification is then experienced though amplified emotion, conscious direction and a third stimulator—spiritual acceleration.

Think of spiritual acceleration as focused time in divine connection. This might typically be experienced in prayer, ceremony or meditation. In this state of Divine reverie a practitioner may slip into bliss or oneness. In both circumstances the spiritual aspirant is in a state beyond time.

The shift from time variance to a curved or spiraled passing of time is what I am most intrigued by. I call this progression 'Spring Theory' and define it as the evolution and progression observed by the human psyche, spirit and emotion moving forward on spiral of advanced development. In this model the observance is what defines the movement of time. As time progresses the observer is moving in a spiral, progressing forward. The linear time model there is the experience of a beginning, middle and end. Spring theory has no sense of a beginning middle or end, but rather all parts are existing at the same moment, and as our human psyche can interpret typically only one part of that greater fullness, we are anchored to a spiral ever in movement towards more understanding and awareness.

Thus the spring, which does continue in a forward movement, is the way we are able to understand or progression. One unique quality that I have frequently had the joy of experiencing in this progression is as we make our passage on the spiral we may dip into the past, or bend into the future. As one routinely passes by their experiences of the past, they can dip into the information once again to release, let go or transform the understanding and knowledge of the previous time. You will gain a new wisdom and understanding to now resolve or release the past, or stretch up into the future, glimpsing at what is to come, or perhaps borrowing from the wisdom and knowledge you haven't yet reached on the spiral, but need in your current life.

## Part Two

My students often ask me: 'where do cycles and timelines come from and why they exist? Do they have purpose?'

This is a good beginning to the conversation. Timelines in a non linear progression would allow you to cycle back or forward to resolve with greater wisdom and understanding that which was incomprehensible or unresolvable in a past experience.

It also allows for a reach into the future to access knowledge you would gain along your path, but have not yet gathered this wisdom based on your location on the progressing spiral.

Have you ever had the feeling of déjà vu? It feels as if you are focused on something that had happened in the past yet it has somehow jumped into your awareness as if it were repeating, both in feeling and in imagery at the present moment.

This phenomenon can be explained by Spiral or Spring theory: which defines our progression of time as forward moving on an upward spiral. Progression of time is not linear but moves in a circular spiral pattern.

What I noticed about this phenomenon was it felt ever evolving but at times the spring seemed to bend down very close to a former period of time in life. As if the experience of time was briefly on a past part of the spiral. During this brief shift an opportunity would emerge to relive or resolve an issue from the past.

In the same way as this shift into the past might occur, at times it would seem to reach up to a future time allowing the shifting experience to provide access to knowledge or wisdom beyond the observer's current scope. This gifting of future knowledge allows for a fast 'upload' than the brilliant revelation seems gone in an instant. This glimpse of brilliance if the viewer of time is open to and ready for a quantum shift may stimulate exponential leaps catapulting the individual out of the present dilemma what ever that may be, to an entirely new experience of life. The gifting of future revelation on the non-linear spiral may provide opportunities beyond the comprehension of the human mind. It could be interpreted as a spiritual awakening. This glimpse into what will be, even if not ready to receive gives courage and proof of that which is not accepted as real in the every day plane of existence. Time as we know it is not the only measure of and in our life, but in our dimension where life is defined by birth, childhood, teenage years, adulthood, retirement, old age and death it would be challenging to imagine a world where everything exists at once, past present and future and time rather then moving from one point to another, might be experienced all at once.

As Humans, spirit in body experience the astrology of cycles, the passage daily of the sun and moon also validate the concept of a circular or spiral of time passing.

Several years back I traveled to the ancient site of underground stone temples of Ireland. The ancients 4500 years ago knew about these spirals and carved them into stone. These spirals help them create the passing of time related to the progression of the sun, and at the equinox the sun would light the inner sanctum of the underground temple, where ceremony was held to send their leaders back to the heavenly realms. I wrote about this experience after observing it.

## The Stones

The stones they are a calling me
Echoing through a eternity
Calling out to set us free
The power of the stones
At dawn I walked in a circle of stones
A solar temple to me yet unknown
Till by the strength of first mornings light
Shown the power of the Stonehenge stones
They grounded the energy of this place
And held us together in loving embrace
While beings of light danced above the space
Bestowing on us their wisdom and grace
The Avebury stones were laughing at me
Taunting me tempting me dancing with glee
Playful stones make love to me
In the circle of the stones
The heavenly chambers from days of old
New Grange stones were a circle to behold
I knelt in prayerful reverence
For the power of the basin stone
I touched my forehead to the rock
It filled me with bright light and talk
Of the ancient people and their ways
And the spirals of the stones
Stones are everywhere we look
Medicine wheels and monolithic books
The wisdom of the circle flows
In the temple of the stones

—2002

The ancients of peoples of England, Scotland and Ireland knew the power of spirals and embedded them in stone to leave us a message to ponder for all of time. From my connecting with the stones I saw the memories in the stones of the ancients. They were actively involved and experimenting with understanding how spirit lives and connects in body and time was an important element to their research. The spirals appear to be a calendar of a sort.

I saw through the memories of the monolithic stones that these humans lived shorter lives than ours probably 45 years of age on the outside. They were involved in creating stone temples that would activate light and time. The equinox and solstice times were sacred times of Divine connection and transition. Divine realms were open and accessible to the ancients during these magical earth cycles.

The 750-year-old yogi Babaji also knew about these spirals. In training given to his inner circle he explained cell rejuvenation in an extraordinary way. As one focus on a sacred mantra like om namah shivah one imagines the cell once moving forward in a spiral motion now reversing its trajectory and moving in a counter clockwise motion.

If we look at it with our quantum field activation to grow cells younger would require you to imagine the master cell moving in a counterclockwise or backwards spiral as you chant. This was his secret to long life and he taught this would ensure the reversal of age.

Humanity as a race has continued to experiment with time bending shape-altering experiences and in each era we are able to master unique transformations supported by the era.

## Part Three

Discovering access to the timeline that flows in a spiral motion though amplified emotion, spiritual acceleration and amplification is one of the most typical ways in. In the supporting field of amplification Humanity as a race has continued to experiment with time bending, shape shifting and altering experiences.

What history reveals is that the age we progress through, like the Piscean or Aquarian age brings special blessings and gift to master. In each era we are able to learn and own for ourselves if we are dedicated to the gift—a unique transformation that is supported by that era.

In this era, which is the age of androgyny, the Aquarian age, our opportunity of transformation is to step into our 'Godself' and own the power of creation. Our cells alighten and awaken in the passage of our timeline in spiral direction. What is so exciting is that if the spiral and Godself skills are used properly an individual can release that which is embedded or stuck in the physical body, your etheric body or even your spirit. This transformation helps one push forward and evolve to the very best expression of self.

In this best expression of self we are the expression of God on the planet. With this kind of power that our thoughts progress out of our mind to become thought forms and ultimately turn into things. The law of attraction and amplification field empower our thoughts and worlds to become our reality. The I am expression from scripture declares what ever we say about ourselves is what we ultimately manifest in our life.

Now, more than ever we must guard against negative thinking and move towards focusing on that which is beautiful, filled with grace, love, charity and compassion so that what is generated from our field is supporting our efforts to evolve.

When a sadness, grief, frustration or anger surface—it's a perfect opportunity to release and let go. As you claim your power of love and peace you let the divine guide and transform your essence to your pure essential nature. There is an incredible power in knowing that you are here as the full and complete  expression of all good. You are the expression of God in physical form. You are here for love, joy and for bliss. You are here to manifest your version of God living and fulfilling full self expression.

What I've learned from my own challenging life is that the things that you suffer through are the things that are not real. This may sound odd, you ay say no they are real my pet died, my husband left me, I was fired from my job and have been out of work for sometime… yes this is part of the 'reality' what I call the game on the planet. But there is indeed a higher dimension, where this suffering makes sense as part of the unfolding plan of awakening. You move out of suffering rapidly if you give no energy to the problem but only focus on and praise all that is right in your life.

You can choose to energize the problem for as long as you need, and you can put an end to suffering rapidly by stepping up to a higher version of your plan. If you believe in and came to know except pain and suffering as a definition of self, then declare; "this is me, I am my pain, I am the abuse, I am what was done to me, I am the illness that I survived, I am the problem you cast a powerful spell upon yourself which you will live in until you are ready to let go and experience union again with the Divine.

By putting aside the struggle or pain and saying: "I am a radiant being of light," "I am fully capable of transforming and healing anything that surfaces," "I am one with the Divine," you will speak a powerful truth into a reality and move into the vibration of enlightenment.

# THESE ARE THE THiNGS OUR ATTORNEY WANTS US TO SHARE WiTH YOU

The content case studies and examples in this book do not in any way represent the "average" or "typical" member experience. In fact, with any program offering a way to improve health, vitality, wealth and love, we know that some members purchase our systems and never use them, and therefore, get no results from their membership at all. You should assume that you will obtain no results from this program. Therefore, the member case studies we are sharing can neither represent nor guarantee the experience of past, current or future program participants or members. Rather, these unique case studies represent what is possible with our system. Each of these unique case studies, and any and all results reported in these case studies by individual members, are the culmination of numerous variables, many of which we cannot control, including; pre-existing mental, emotional and health conditions, personal incentive, discontinuity of spiritual and energetic conditions and countless other tangible and intangible factors.

Whether this notice refers to 'you' or 'your' it means you while 'we' or 'our' refers to Gable-Kennedy Inc. dba 100% You.

Any improvements in health, mindset and energy are examples of what we think you can achieve. There are no assurances you'll do as well. If you rely only on the assurances in this book you must accept the risk of not doing as well.

Where specific health activations that have for others returned their health to high function, these examples are used and attributed to the individuals/ participants who have experienced these shifts, through 100% Healthy individual and group programs. There is no assurance you will do as well. If you rely on our 'transformations' you must also assume the risk of not doing as well.

Any representation of improved health, wealth, relationship and mindset in this book, our websites and in our programs are not considered to be average or normal. Likewise any claims or representations from our course participants and students are not considered to be average results.

There can be no assurances that any prior successes or past results regarding health, wealth, love and relationships can be used as an indication of future success or results.

Returning health, energy, clarity and ease to the body are based on many factors. We have no way of knowing how well you will do, as we do not know you, your background, your ability to heal, your 'work' ethics or basic health and body care practices. Therefore, we do not guarantee or imply that you will have improvements or achieve better health, wealth, relationships, love, money or any other improvements suggested in this book, on our website or anywhere else. If you rely only on the assurances in this book you must accept the risk of not doing as well.

100% Healthy and 100% You programs are designed for people who are already healthy and want to take their health to the next level. Your health, wealth and love are entirely in your hands. Our programs are meant to be educational in nature and these programs may not be suited for everyone. Making decisions based on any information presented in our products, services or website should be done only with the knowledge that you could experience significant losses or make no improvements at all, or achieve no desired results regarding health, wealth, relationships, and energy.

Use caution and seek the advice of qualified professionals. Check with your health care director, therapist or professional business advisor, before acting on this or any information.

Users of our products, services and website are advised to do their own due diligence when it comes to making health decisions and all information, products and services that have been provided should be independently verified by your own qualified professional. Our information, products and services on www. julierenee.com should be carefully considered and evaluated, before reaching a business decision on whether to rely on them.

You agree that our companies are not responsible for the success or failure of your health, wealth or relationship decisions relating to the information presented by www.julierenee.com or our companies' products or services.

# FROM iLLNESS TO WORLD RENOWNED MENTOR: JULiE RENEE'S STORY

As a child I was exposed to the cruelest health killer imaginable; Atomic radiation. As you can imagine I experienced the worst possible health conditions known to humankind, from multiple cancers, a year in a wheel chair and even death itself. This difficult passage took many, many years of my life, actually years in a hospital bed; with no doctor thinking I would live another day. Yet even when faced with death I refused to die. I said to the angel of death 'get thee behind me Satan... I know you're not Satan, but I'm not coming with you', and the angel of death left.

Eight years ago I found myself fatigued and exhausted. I was almost ready to give up the fight. I was emotionally discouraged that I had not been able to get my bigger message out into the world, nor had I been able to enjoy the journey of life. My adrenals were fried, my brain in a constant fog; my life, even by my account, was not worth living anymore. Now that's pretty bad, I am an optimist by nature, but I couldn't imagine going another day in the kind of suffering and exhaustion I was in. They say it's always darkest before the dawn, and that was a dark week. Then I began to awaken from my own illusion. I woke one morning with absolute certainty that God had promised me a Garden of Eden life and that I needed to collect.

I went to my own little garden in prayer and meditation and just like Buddha, determined for my own enlightenment, I demanded God take me or make me well. From that very first day I began to receive downloads of regeneration and the human blueprint. I had access to how we were designed, and how we were meant to live hundreds of years based on our design. My body began to regenerate (heal) and after two short weeks I had no pain in my body. Within a few weeks, I who had previously walked with a cane, had asthma and a heart condition, could now run the mountain trails and dance on stage with a local rock 'n roll band.

## Developing the Mission: 5,000,000 Minds!

It was fascinating to me to understand each and every process, (I'm a combination of class president and actress for those of you who know about character codes) and I was driven to learn more and more. When I had really healed my own body to a large extent, I started to use the techniques I had developed with my clients. The fascination grew to a magnificent obsession and I began to apply the principles to the profoundly ill folks who were coming in droves to experience my regeneration gifts. I was saving lives. WOW.

As I worked with the ill folks, I realized my real desire was to return to the women; the ladies who were going for it. I found myself mentoring and restoring health with woman leaders, housewives and wise elders who were still very much involved in the transforming planet! A consistent thread was all these women wanted more, they refused to play small but so often were being held back because of exhaustion, healthy issues, and the demands of overly active schedules. I found myself taking these  amazing women leaders from sometimes total depletion to absolute miraculous break through! As time has progressed, I have learned so much more in mentoring women and men all ages to live richer deeper lives. As I progressed I realized that we could as a race restore the wellness and purity of our human blueprint by reaching and aligning five million minds!

I found a common thread with my tribe. First off they were brilliant. They were awake and aware, meaning they knew that life isn't just black and white, there is a spiritual component to things, and not everything that affects your success is seen or visible. Self-accountability was another key to these amazing women. They sometimes accepted responsibility for things that were failing in their life, even though they had no awareness of where the problem stemmed from or how to 'fix' it.

When they came to me, they were exhausted and smart enough to know they needed help to keep up their momentum. I would hear over and over, "Julie Renee I don't want to work so hard, I feel like things should get easier, that I should be feeling a sense of joy and balance". Then I would hear about the problem and how they couldn't afford to play small. "I feel like I am stuck on a hamster wheel. On my days off I am so tired I crash, it's not uncommon for me to sleep well into the afternoon. I am embarrassed that I can't remember important facts, details and names when I am so tired. To make matters worse, with my fuzzy brain I can't write, so I am behind on my book writing commitments."

They asked me if it was possible to have momentum without the struggle and effort? Could they be happy? Could they feel energized and healthy like they did before they started to really go for it? Would they ever be able to return to sleeping well at night?

Yes. Yes. Yes.

# PRECiOUS ADViCE JUST FOR YOU FROM JULiE RENEE

Dear One,

I am so grateful for you in my life and for allowing me the opportunity to assist you in moving towards a life of freedom and joy. Creating this program has been a pleasure as I have pulled together teachings from the recent seven years of my now 22 year career in mentoring and activating health to 100%!

Let me help you take your next step.

You've gotten a lot of great information in this book and hopefully a lot of value too. If you're like me you'll want to learn how you can take this work to the next level and get your life skyrocketing with better health, energy, connection and momentum.

Since no two people are exactly alike, I'd like to suggest three choices on ways to take your pursuit of Quantum Healing into your life. Keep in mind I have been teaching and assisting folks with health for more than two decades and am prolific. I encourage you to explore the JulieRenee.com website and discover a wealth of mini programs and directed meditations if you would like to jump in with baby steps.

If, however, you like to take action in a big way and are ready to have it all, here are the three paths to choose from:

100% You Quiz: Take the 100% You Assessment—get immediate results and a free program!

Fatigue to Fabulous program: Clear out Stress and Rejuvenate Your System!

7 Day Accelerate Wealth: This FREE program is particularly for people with little money and wanting quick shifts!

# ABOUT THE AUTHOR

Julie Renee refuses to play small. She powerfully mentors those who are being taken out of the game with exhaustion and "fuzzy brain." She regenerates the brain and gets them back to playing at 100% again.

Books by Julie Renee are 100% You, Your Divine Human Blueprint, and Balance Your Life Now!

Julie Renee is the founder and developer of a new spiritual science, the 100% Healthy Human Blueprint. She is the author of the groundbreaking book, Your Divine Human Blueprint. Her unique gift of healing defines the energy-science of Cellular Quantum Mechanics. She trains individuals in her "100% You Immersion Program" and sees private VIP clients in her home in northern California.

After launching her first business from her tiny San Francisco studio apartment in 1993, she has prevailed over a challenging history of multiple cancers and five near-death experiences. Overcoming tremendous odds, none of her doctors saw a possibility for her to survive her illnesses; she was repeatedly told she    was dying. Unwilling to believe that this was true, even the Angel of Death could not convince her that it was her time to go. She has dedicated her life to the betterment of humankind and the reawakening of humanity to the Divine Human Blueprint.

Recognized for her leadership abilities, she is the recipient of the 2010-2011 National Association of Professional Women's "Woman of the Year Award" and the Powerful Women International's "Global Leadership Award" 2012.

Julie Renee has been featured as an expert on CBS, Unity FM, Rock Star Radio, Blog Talk Align, Live 365, Low Down, Spirit Seeker, 11: 11 Magazine, Spirit Seeker Magazine, and on various TV shows, including "New Era Healing" and a "Forum on Spirituality." She is a writer for Holistic Fashionista Magazine and Accomplish Magazine. She is also the host of the radio show, 100% Healthy. Additionally, she has both stage and film credits, and is a harpist and singer.

Julie Renee is the 100% Healthy Life EXPERT. She helps women succeed in life and business by activating them simply and easily to get to 100% in both health and vitality. An expert meditation instructor, she shares the secrets of altering reality through meditation, and provides an integrated fast track for manifesting, holding and growing abundance, health, beauty, and wealth. Her home activation programs include the following:

- Beautiful From the Inside Out
- Accelerate Wealth 21 - Day Program
- Illumination Rosary for Enlightenment
- The Sound of Truth - Vedic Mantra for transformation
- Your Secret Keys audio series
- The Definitive Guide to Meditation series
- Your Divine Human Blueprint home study audio series
- Unlimited Love

As a speaker, she has shared the stage with Marci Shimoff, Jack Canfield, Caterina Rando, James Malinchak, Sean Aston, Stedman Graham, Julie Carrier, Dr. Bill Dorfman, Jill Lublin, PJ Van Hulle, and many others.

## From Farm Wife to Health Activator

Julie Renee started out in Minnesota as a farm wife, attended art school, modeled, waitressed, appeared in seven films, became a very successful realtor, and finally moved into her passion as a healer in the form of a health activator. She now has over thirty years' experience supporting individuals and groups in Quantum Health Activations, from high-risk pregnancies to life-saving interventions with critically ill individuals. Known as the premier healer for high risk pregnancies, twenty doctors and six midwives sent their most difficult clients to Julie Renee to help them from gestation through the first year after birth. In all, she has assisted more than one hundred and forty high risk babies to successfully enter this world.

Many years ago, she taught yoga and offered healing massage to people in recovery. She also taught infant massage, worked with insurance companies, and helped injured clients return to living, and hospice clients pass from this world, pain-free and without medication as they said good-by to their loved ones.

Moving deeper into her exploration of regeneration, she developed specialized Jadeite hot stone treatments, accessing the knowledge of the ancient civilizations of the Olmecs and Mayans, who used Jadeite for body initiations and transformations.

As part of a natural progression, Julie Renee moved from physical healing to offering spiritual life coaching for women. Through her clairvoyant gifts, she helped women rapidly shift to move into their next highest step.

For the past seven years, Julie Renee has been researching and developing programs with the Blueprint, teaching through guidebooks, courses and meditation as a simple way to access the healing gifts and secrets of the Divine Human Blueprint.

Thousands of individuals have created health, wealth and love with Julie Renee's help. Through her extraordinary gifts, she has brought critically ill people back into their lives, restoring health to their cellular and energetic bodies through the Divine Human Blueprint.

Traveling the world, she has studied in India, and is both an ordained minister and a pujari (carrier of the light) in the yogic tradition.

Julie Renee's favorite vacations include rappelling down waterfalls, zip lining, and performing daring acts, such as shooting down the longest water slide in Mexico. She loves the ocean, the mountains, and nature, and is a nature girl at heart. You can find her out hiking trails every chance she gets. She challenges herself regularly by rappelling, and doing other fun but scary activities that involve hanging from great heights with ropes. Her favorite ice cream is rose petal. She loves mangos and scented flowers, especially garden roses.

Julie Renee can be reached through her website at:
www.JulieRenee.com
or on any of the following social sites: Facebook, YouTube, LinkedIn, Twitter, and Pinterest

Made in the USA
San Bernardino, CA
07 April 2017